Child and Adolescent Mental Health Series

FOCUS

Cannabis and Young People

Reviewing the Evidence

Richard Jenkins

The Royal College of
Psychiatrists 2006

Jessica Kingsley Publishers
London and Philadelphia

First published in 2006
by Jessica Kingsley Publishers
116 Pentonville Road
London N1 9JB, UK
and
400 Market Street, Suite 400
Philadelphia, PA 19106, USA

www.jkp.com

Library of Congress Cataloging in Publication Data
Cannabis and young people : reviewing the evidence / Richard Jenkins.
   p. cm. -- (Child and adolescent mental health series)
Includes bibliographical references and index.
ISBN-13: 978-1-84310-398-1 (pbk. : alk. paper)
ISBN-10: 1-84310-398-2 (pbk. : alk. paper)
   1. Youth--Drug use. 2. Marijuana.   I. Title. II. Series.
HV5824.Y68J46 2006
616.86'350083--dc22

                                                            2005031638

British Library Cataloguing in Publication Data
A CIP catalogue record for this book is available from the British Library

ISBN-13: 978 1 84310 398 1
ISBN-10: 1 84310 398 2

Printed and bound in Great Britain by
Athenaeum Press, Gateshead, Tyne and Wear

Contents

1 Introduction

Cannabis has been the subject of considerable and often impassioned debate over the years. In 1967, *The Times* newspaper included a full-page advertisement signed by a variety of public figures, including the Beatles, that called for a review of the drug's legal status (IDMU 2005). Opinion on the potential consequences of cannabis use is sharply divided, with some arguing that it poses serious risks to both physical and mental health, while others believe that any effects are modest by comparison with those of alcohol or tobacco (Wodak, Reinarman and Cohen 2002). A survey of over 1600 adults in the UK conducted by MORI in 1999 found that, although a majority of respondents wanted stronger drug laws, half of those questioned agreed that the law should be changed so that it was no longer illegal to use cannabis (Pearson and Shiner 2002).

Public discussion on the topic has intensified in the UK following the Home Office's reclassification of cannabis as a Class C substance under the Misuse of Drugs Act in January 2004 (Home Office 2005). The production, supply and possession of cannabis remain illegal, although the maximum penalties have been reduced from five years' to two years' imprisonment. For young people under the age of 18, a first offence of possession results in an arrest and a formal warning or reprimand, with further offences leading to a final warning or charge. At the time of writing, however, the reclassification policy was being reviewed (BBC 2005a) following the publication of recent research demonstrating an association between cannabis use in adolescence and the reporting of psychotic symptoms in young adulthood (Fergusson, Horwood and Ridder 2005; Henquet *et al.* 2005).

In the light of these developments, the purpose of this book is to review the evidence on a range of issues relating to the use of cannabis among children and adolescents. Patterns of cannabis use are examined, drawing upon the latest prevalence figures from international and national surveys, together with findings from a number of large-scale cohort studies documenting changes in usage (e.g. from experimental to regular and higher frequency use) over the course of adolescence. Young people's views about cannabis, including their assessment of its potential harmful effects in comparison with other substances and their reasons for using the drug, are also discussed. The findings from various longitudinal studies are summarised to highlight the individual, family and social factors that predict the initiation of cannabis use in adolescence, the progression to regular use and the likelihood of cessation in young adulthood. The review also includes the potential effects of cannabis use including mental health problems, other aspects of psychosocial functioning such as educational attainment and antisocial behaviour, and the use of other illicit drugs. Studies evaluating the effects of prevention programmes and treatment interventions, and the impact of changes in cannabis policy such as 'decriminalisation', are also considered.

Literature search strategy

Studies of cannabis use among children and adolescents, published from 1990 onwards, were identified from a search of the Cochrane Library and the Cinahl, Embase, Medline and Psycinfo bibliographic databases. The search was originally conducted in December 2004 and updated in March 2005. The titles and abstracts of the retrieved citations were assessed for their relevance to the research topics addressed by each of this book's main chapters. Full text articles of the relevant citations were then obtained for critical appraisal, and their reference lists were checked for any additional relevant articles.

Wherever possible, existing systematic reviews, meta-analyses or other detailed literature reviews formed the basis of the evidence for each of the research topics. Individual studies were then considered according to a 'hierarchy of evidence' reflecting the robustness of their methodological designs (Khan *et al.* 2003). For example, the review of evidence examining the association between cannabis use and psychosocial functioning concentrated on longitudinal cohort studies that featured prospective measures of cannabis use and statistical analyses controlling for the effects of confounding variables. Prevention programmes and treatment interventions were evaluated primarily in terms of randomised controlled trials or RCTs. These involve the random allocation of participants to an intervention or control group, with follow-up assessments to examine differences in the outcomes between the groups. The process of randomisation is designed to balance the groups for known as well as unknown variables that may have an impact on the final outcomes.

Cannabis terminology

The term 'cannabis' refers to several products that may be obtained from the cannabis or hemp plant (Drugscope 2005). Cannabis resin (hashish, hash) is the secretion from the flowering tops of the plant, which is then pressed into brown or black blocks. Herbal cannabis (marijuana, grass, ganga) is the dried flower-bearing stems and top shoots of the plant, and sometimes also the leaves and parts of the stem. Cannabis oil is a thick, brown or black liquid that is made by percolating a solvent through the resin. The psychoactive effects of cannabis are caused by chemical substances known as cannabinoids, the most potent type being tetra-hydrocannabinol (THC) (Ashton 2001).

2 Patterns of Cannabis Use

Prevalence of use

International surveys

Two of the main sources of international data on the prevalence of cannabis use among children and adolescents are the Health Behaviour in School-aged Children study (HBSC) and the European School Survey Project on Alcohol and Other Drugs (ESPAD). To date, there have been six HBSC surveys, collecting data on a range of health topics from school pupils aged 11, 13 and 15 years. The latest available findings are from the 2001/02 survey, which involved 35 countries and other territories in Europe and North America (Currie *et al.* 2004). Questions on cannabis use were included for the first time, although for the 15-year-old age group only, on the grounds that use of the drug is infrequent among children and early adolescents. The sample size of respondents in this age group ranged from 240 in Greenland to 2614 in France, with 15 countries achieving the target of 1500 pupils. The 2001/02 survey showed that the proportion of 15-year-olds across all the HBSC countries who had used cannabis at least once during their lives was 25.8% in the case of males and 18.9% for females. Of these respondents, 7.3% were classified as 'experimental' users (one to two times), 7.9% reported 'recreational' use (three to 39 times) and 2.8% were 'heavy' users (40 or more times). Heavy users comprised between 5 and 10% of the samples in Canada, England, Scotland, Spain, Switzerland and the US. In all countries, heavy use was more common among boys than girls. Use of the drug during the previous year ranged from a low of 3% in the former Yugoslav Republic of Macedonia to a high of 40% in Canada. Over 30% of pupils in England,

Greenland, Scotland, Spain, Switzerland and the US reported past-year use of the drug. Overall, cannabis use across the HBSC countries was more common among boys (21.7%) than girls (16%).

The ESPAD documents the level of substance use across Europe among school pupils who are, or will become, 16 years old during the year of data collection. The first survey, involving 26 countries, was completed in 1995, the second in 1999 and the latest in 2003, featuring over 100,000 pupils from 35 countries (ESPAD 2005). The number of participants in each country ranged from 555 in Greenland to almost 6000 in Poland, although in most cases the sample size was close to or above the recommended target of 2400. In 2003, the Czech Republic had the highest 'lifetime' prevalence rate of marijuana or hashish use, with 44% reporting use of the drug at least once during their lives. High rates were also reported in Switzerland (40%), Ireland (39%), the Isle of Man (39%), France (38%) and the UK (38%). The lowest levels (under 5%) were for Cyprus, Romania and Turkey. The country with the highest proportion of pupils using the drug during the last month was France (22%), followed by the Isle of Man (21%), Switzerland (20%) and the UK (20%). The lowest levels (under 5%) were reported in Cyprus, the Faroe Islands, Finland, Greece, Iceland, Latvia, Malta, Norway, Romania, Sweden and Turkey. In most ESPAD countries, cannabis use was more common among boys than girls.

Surveys of use in the UK

A series of surveys have been conducted on behalf of the Department of Health since 1982 to examine the prevalence of health-related behaviours among 11- to 15-year-old school pupils in England. Questions on illegal drug use were first included in 1998. The latest available data on cannabis use are from the 2004 survey, involving a sample of nearly 10,000 pupils from 313 schools across the country (Department of Health 2005). In 2004, 11% of pupils reported using cannabis at least once during the previous year, compared with 13% in the 2001, 2002 and 2003 surveys. Prevalence was slightly higher among boys (12%) than girls (10%) and increased with age, from 1% of 11-year-olds to 7% of 13-year-olds and 26% of 15-year-olds.

The 2004 Scottish Schools Adolescent Lifestyle and Substance Use Survey (SALSUS) details the prevalence of smoking, drinking and substance use among secondary 2 and 4 grade pupils (i.e. mainly 13- and 15-year-olds, respectively) in Scotland (Corbett *et al.* 2005). A total of 340 classes in 194 schools participated, with 7062 pupils completing questionnaires. Cannabis use in the year prior to the survey was reported by 10% of 13-year-olds and 28% of 15-year-olds. For use in the previous month, the figures were 7% of 13-year-old boys and 5% of 13-year-old girls, rising to 20% of 15-year-old boys and 18% of 15-year-old girls.

The HBSC provides the latest data on cannabis use among adolescents across Wales, with the 2001/02 survey involving approximately 1500 15-year-old school pupils (Currie *et al.* 2004). The proportion of the sample reporting the use of cannabis in the last year was 26% for boys and 24% for girls. Among the HBSC countries, Wales was ranked tenth highest, with England third and Scotland seventh. Three per cent of the Welsh sample who reported cannabis use at least once during their lives were classified as heavy users (40 or more times), compared with 6% in Scotland and 7% in England.

The use of cannabis among school children in Northern Ireland was documented in the 2003 Young Person's Behaviour and Attitudes Survey, which collected data on a range of health and social issues from a sample of 7223 students, aged 11 to 16, in 74 schools (Central Survey Unit 2005). Just over 13% reported using cannabis at some point during the previous year, with 8.5% using the drug in the last month and 4.5% in the last week.

One important limitation of these school-based surveys is the lack of detailed figures on substance use among different ethnic groups. To address this issue, Rodham *et al.* (2005) examined ethnic differences in the prevalence of a number of health-related behaviours, including drug taking, among a sample of 15- to 16-year-old pupils from schools in Oxfordshire, Northamptonshire and Birmingham. Sixty-four schools, varying in terms of their size, type (state, grammar or independent), gender (single sex or co-educational), educational attainment, socio-economic deprivation and ethnic composition, were asked to participate and 41 agreed to do so. A total of 6020 pupils completed questionnaires on substance use and recorded their ethnic status from a list of four categories ('White', 'Asian', 'Black' or 'Other'). The ethnic composition of the sample was similar to that for England as a whole, except for a greater proportion of pupils describing themselves as being of Asian origin. Among male pupils, the reporting of cannabis use in the past year was more common among those describing their ethnic status as 'Black' (49.3%) or 'Other' (44.3%) than White (33.5%). Asian pupils of both genders were the least likely of the four ethnic categories to report past-year cannabis use (21.5% of males and 5.5% of females).

An additional criticism of school-based surveys is that they are likely to underestimate the true extent of substance use, since drug-taking is typically higher among adolescents who truant or are excluded from school (Lloyd 1998; Miller and Plant 1999). Cannabis use among these two groups was examined by the Youth Lifesyles Survey 1998/99, involving a sample of 4848 young people, aged 12 to 30, in England and Wales (Goulden and Sondhi 2001). Figures for school truants (truanting from school for a whole day in the past year without permission) and excluded pupils (missing school at least one day per term or expelled/suspended at some point during their school career) were recorded for the 12 to 16 age group. The proportions reporting cannabis use during the past year were 42% in the case of truants and 34% of excluded pupils, compared with 8% of pupils attending school on a regular basis. With regard to gender differences, cannabis use during the last year was significantly higher among female truants (52%) compared with males (32%). Excluded female pupils also reported significantly higher cannabis use (52%) than males (29%).

The main sources of information about the prevalence of illegal drug use among older adolescents (age 16 and over) in the UK are from household surveys such as the British Crime Survey (BCS). The BCS samples a representative cross-section of 16- to 59-year-olds living in private households in England and Wales. In addition to asking respondents about their experiences of crime, the survey has included questions on the use of illicit drugs since 1996. The 2002/03 survey found that just under a quarter (24.6%) of 16- to 19-year-olds had used cannabis in the past year and 15.3% had used the drug in the previous month (Condon and Smith 2003). In the 2003 Scottish Crime Survey (McVie, Campbell and Lebov 2004), 21% of 16- to 19-year-olds in Scotland reported past-year cannabis use, with a higher rate among males (25%) than females (15.7%). The Drug Prevalence Survey, covering Northern Ireland and the Irish Republic, was conducted for the first time in 2002/03, involving a representative sample of 15- to 64-year-olds who were normally resident in private households (NACD and DAIRU 2003). The final achieved sample for Northern Ireland was 3517, representing a response rate of 63%. Among the 15- to 24-year-old age group, 12% of respondents reported use of cannabis in the past year and 8% stated that they had used the drug in the last month.

Household surveys are a useful indicator of how many adolescents have tried cannabis but they often lack information on the frequency and other aspects of use. A questionnaire study by McCambridge and Strang (2004a) provided a more detailed picture of cannabis use among a sample of 200 young people attending 10 further education colleges in inner London. The participants were aged 16 to 20 and all were currently involved in illegal drug use on more than an occasional basis, defined as a minimum of weekly cannabis use and/or current stimulant drug use within the previous three months. Ninety-six participants (48% of the sample) stated that they used cannabis either every day or nearly every day, with an average of 26.6 episodes of use per week. Sixty-two partici-pants (31%) reported weekly (but not daily) use of the drug, with an average of 6.6 episodes of use per week. The most common form of cannabis used was 'grass' (49%), followed by 'skunk' (36%). Almost half of the sample (49%) stated that all, or nearly all, of their friends used cannabis, and 45% reported that they never, or almost never, used cannabis alone.

Like school-based studies, household surveys of substance use are also prone to underestimating the level of substance use in the general population, as they do not sample groups such as the homeless or young offenders. The prevalence of cannabis use among the young homeless in four areas of England and Wales (Birmingham, Brighton and Hove, Can-terbury and Cardiff) was documented in a report from the UK Home Office Drug Research Programme (Wincup, Buckland and Bayliss 2003). Data were collected from a total of 160 young people, aged 25 and under, recruited through homelessness agencies. Cannabis use in the past year was reported by 80% of the 35 respondents aged 16 to 17. In another

Home Office report, Hammersley, Marsland and Reid (2003) examined substance use among a sample of 293 young people aged 12 to 18 from 11 youth offending teams across England and Wales. Eighty six per cent of the sample reported using cannabis at least once during their lives, with 71% having used it in the last four weeks. Of those who had used cannabis at some point during the previous year, 71% were classified as 'heavier' users (25 to 365 times).

Changes in use over time

A number of large-scale, longitudinal cohort studies have provided information on changes in the patterns of cannabis use during the course of adolescence, such as the proportion of individuals who go on to become regular users or develop dependence on the drug.

Christchurch Health and Development Study (CHDS)

The CHDS comprises a cohort of 1265 children born in the Christchurch urban region of New Zealand in mid-1977 (Fergusson and Horwood 2001). The cohort has been assessed at birth, four months, one year, at annual intervals until age 16 years, and again at 18, 21 and 25 years.

Fergusson and Horwood (2000a) describe the development of cannabis use in the Christchurch cohort up to the age of 21 years. Cohort members were questioned about their cannabis use in terms of the age at which they first used the drug and an estimate of the frequency of use in each year from age 14 to 21. These yearly estimates were summed to give an estimate of the respondent's cumulative cannabis use during this period. Cannabis use increased markedly with age, from 9.3% of respondents at age 15 to 49.8% of 18-year-olds and 68.9% at age 21. From the age of 17 onwards, use of the drug was more common among males than females. There were considerable variations in the frequency of cannabis use, with around a quarter of respondents reporting use on fewer than 10 occasions during the period from ages 14 to 21 and 4.7% using it on more than 400 occasions. High frequency use was more common among males (8.3%) than females (1.3%).

Dunedin Multidisciplinary Health and Development Study (DMHDS)

The DMHDS is a longitudinal investigation of the health, development and behaviour of a large sample of New Zealand children followed from birth to adulthood (Silva and Stanton 1996). The children were part of a cohort born between 1 April 1972 and 31 March 1973 and first enrolled in the study at the age of 3, with an initial sample size of 1037. Assessments involving a range of psychological, medical and sociological measures were conducted every two years until the age of 15, and again at 18, 21 and 26 years.

Poulton *et al.* (1997) examined changes in cannabis use among the DMHDS cohort from the age of 15 to 21 years. As part of a general mental health assessment, cohort members were questioned about their use of cannabis in the previous 12 months at the ages of 15, 18 and 21. At age 15, the proportion of the sample reporting past-year use was 15%, which rose to 43.4% (46.7% for males, 40% for females) at age 18 and 52.4% (58.6% for males, 46.1% for females) three years later. There were no gender differences in terms of 'intermittent' use (defined as less than six times) at ages 18 and 21, although significantly more males than females reported 'frequent' use (six or more times) at age 18.

Of those reporting cannabis use at age 21, approximately one-third had been non-users at age 18. About a quarter of 18-year-olds classified as 'intermittent' users, and approximately 10% of 'frequent' users, had stopped using the drug by age 21. During the period from age 15 to 21, females were more likely than males to remain non-users or low frequency users. Early 'frequent' use was strongly related to later use, with all males classified as 'frequent' users at 15 continuing to use the drug at age 21.

Early Developmental Stages of Psychopathology Study (EDSPS)

The EDSPS examined the prevalence and course of a range of mental disorders, with a particular focus on substance use disorders, among a randomly selected general population sample of 14- to 24-year-olds in Munich, Germany (Wittchen *et al.* 1998b). Data were collected in three stages, beginning in 1995 with follow-up assessments in 1996/97 and

1998/99. A total of 3021 participants were interviewed at the start of the study, with 1395 individuals aged 14 to 17 years.

Perkonigg *et al.* (1999) reported on the findings of the first follow-up assessment, which was conducted an average of 19.7 months later and confined to those cohort members who were aged 14 to 17 at baseline. Cannabis use among the 1228 individuals who participated in this assessment was measured using the Munich version of the Composite International Diagnostic Interview (Lachner, Wittchen and Perkonigg *et al.* 1998). At the beginning of the study, 17.3% of adolescents had reported using cannabis at least once during their lives, with 4.8% having tried it only once, 6.4% two to four times (classified as 'repeated' use) and 6.1% five times or more ('regular' use). By the time of the follow-up assessment, however, 32.5% of the sample (34.8% of males and 30.2% of females) had tried the drug, with 5.2% reporting a single use, 9.7% repeated use and 17.8% regular use. Just under a fifth (18.6%) of adolescents who were non-users at baseline reported cannabis use during the follow-up period, with 3.5% trying it only once, 7.8% repeatedly and 7.3% regularly.

For those individuals reporting 'repeated' cannabis use at the start of the study, 26.1% no longer used the drug by the follow-up, while a third (33.3%) continued with their previous pattern of use and the same percentage progressed to 'considerable' use (defined as one to two times a week). Only 17.7% of 'regular' users at baseline stopped using cannabis completely by the follow-up, with nearly three-quarters (74.2%) maintaining regular use at follow-up. Over half the respondents (54.8%) who reported 'considerable' use at the outset continued with this level of use during the follow-up period.

Victorian Adolescent Health Cohort Study

This study featured a sample of students from 44 secondary schools in the Australian state of Victoria (Coffey *et al.* 2000). Two classes were selected at random from each of the schools, with one class entering the study in the latter part of the ninth school year (wave 1) and the second class six months later, early in the tenth year (wave 2). The entire sample of 2032 14- to15-year-olds completed a questionnaire on adolescent health issues, including mental health and lifestyle. Follow-up assessments were conducted at six-month intervals over the next two years (waves 3 to 6), with a final follow-up (wave 7) at the age of 20 to 21 years.

Coffey *et al.* (2000) reported on the frequency of cannabis use reported during the 'mid-school' (waves 2 and 3) and 'late-school' (waves 4 to 6) periods of the study. Twenty-one per cent of the 1864 students providing data in waves 2 and 3 reported using cannabis during the mid-school period, and the majority of these students continued to use the drug into 'late-school'. Although just under a quarter (24.5%) of students who reported less than weekly use in waves 2 and 3 had stopped using cannabis during the late-school period, almost half (47.9%) maintained their earlier pattern of use. Only 4% of weekly users during mid-school had become non-users in the late-school period, with the majority either continuing with weekly use (37.3%) or increasing to daily use (29.3%).

Trajectories of cannabis use

Two recent studies (Ellickson, Martino and Collins 2004a; Windle and Wiesner 2004) have sought to identify discrete patterns or trajectories of cannabis use across the course of adolescence and into young adulthood. Ellickson *et al.* (2004a) analysed data collected over a ten-year period from 5833 participants in the RAND Adolescent/Young Adult Panel Study. The sample was originally recruited from 30 middle schools in the states of California and Oregon, US. Self-administered surveys were completed by the participants in school at grade 7 through to grade 10, by mail at grade 12 and again at the age of 23. Participants who did not report marijuana use at any time during the study were excluded from the analyses.

Four trajectory groups of marijuana users were identified: 'early high', 'stable light', 'occasional light' and 'steady increasers'. Early high users (5% of all participants who reported marijuana use during the ten years) were characterised by a relatively high level of use at the age of 13 (i.e. varying between monthly and weekly use), which then declined until around age 18 and continued at a relatively moderate level (approximately three to ten times a year) into young adulthood. Stable light users (17%) maintained a relatively low level of use, no more than ten times a year on average, throughout adolescence and up to the age of 23. The majority of the sample (53%) was classified as reporting occasional light use of marijuana. This group was similar to the stable light use trajectory but was characterised by no use at the beginning of the study and relatively lower levels of use during the subsequent ten years. A quarter of marijuana users were steady increasers, with no use reported at the age of 13 but increasing their use in a near-linear fashion throughout adolescence until young adulthood, where they reported the highest level of use for all the four trajectory groups. Additional analyses were performed to examine relationships between these trajectories and the frequency with which participants had been offered marijuana, together with their perceived ability to refuse these offers. For the early high users, the decrease in marijuana use after the age of 13 was accompanied by a reduction in the number of offers and an increase in refusal ability, while the steady increasers reported parallel increases in offers and decreases in refusal ability between the ages of 13 and 18.

Windle and Wiesner (2004) analysed data from a predominantly white and middle-class sample of 1205 participants in the Lives Across Time study, which examined risk factors for adolescent substance use. An initial sample of 975 students was recruited from two suburban public high school districts in western New York State, US. Data were first collected when pupils were in the tenth or eleventh grades, followed by three further assessments conducted at six-month intervals. An additional sample of 235 adolescents was recruited at the time of the first follow-up to increase the sample size for some low baseline variables, such as family history of alcoholism.

The analyses of data from the four assessments identified five trajectory groups. The majority of the sample (82.4%) was classified as 'abstainers', with no reports of marijuana in the entire study. 'Experimental users' (8.8%) rarely used the drug during this period, while 'increasers' (3.6%) were characterised by an initial low level of use followed by a steady increase for the remainder of the study. Participants classified as 'decreasers' (3.4%) or 'high chronics' (1.8%) had a relatively high level of marijuana use at the start of the study, but the latter group maintained this level across all four assessments. A comparison of the four trajectories on a variety of psychosocial measures found that high chronic users had significantly higher levels of delinquent activity than any of the other groups. Abstainers had the lowest levels of alcohol use, delinquent activity and stressful life events, and the smallest number of friends who used alcohol or drugs.

Dependence

The fourth edition of the Diagnostic Statistical Manual of Mental Disorders (DSM-IV-TR) defines substance dependence as 'a maladaptive pattern of substance use, leading to clinically significant impairment or distress' (APA 2000, p.197). A diagnosis of dependence requires the occurrence during a 12-month period of three or more symptoms from a list of seven criteria. One example of a diagnosis would be an individual who has been consuming ever increasing amounts of the drug during this period to obtain the same desired effect, has given up or reduced important occupational or social activities as a result of their drug use, and continues to use despite the experiencing of drug-related physical and/or psychological problems.

Although withdrawal is listed among the criteria for substance dependence, DSM-IV comments that the clinical significance of withdrawal symptoms in relation to cannabis use in particular is uncertain (APA 2000). A review of the published literature on this topic (Smith 2002) notes that the pattern, onset, duration and abatement of symptoms among former cannabis users are inconsistent, and that there are a number of alternative explanations of these symptom reports such as underlying mental health conditions or personality traits.

Few studies have documented withdrawal among adolescents. Duffy and Milin (1996) reported three case studies of adolescents, who were assessed by a child and adolescent psychiatrist specialising in addiction psychiatry. All adolescents had a history of chronic heavy cannabis use (at least 2 to 3 grams daily for a period of six months or longer), a diagnosis of cannabis dependence and had developed significant tolerance to the drug. None met the criteria for any other substance abuse or dependence disorder. In each case, the individuals' attempts to reduce or stop using cannabis were accompanied within 48 hours by a range of symptoms, including agitation, shakiness, drug craving, irritable and labile mood, diaphoresis, insomnia, fluctuations in appetite, nausea, vomiting, diarrhoea and gastrointestinal upset. These symptoms finally abated after a period of 10 to 14 days, with insomnia and irritable mood persisting the longest.

Crowley *et al.* (1998) examined the reporting of cannabis withdrawal symptoms among a sample of 229 13- to 19-year-olds who were patients in a university treatment programme for delinquent youths. Participants were selected from the programme population on the basis of having one or more substance dependence diagnoses and three or more lifetime symptoms of conduct disorder. Of the 180 youths diagnosed with cannabis dependence according to DSM-III-R criteria (APA 1987), 121 reported withdrawal, the most common symptoms being 'tired, sleepy, weak' in the case of males (61.1%) and 'affecting appetite' in females (50%). However, the authors acknowledged that poly-drug use among the sample might have resulted in the misidentification of symptoms as cannabis withdrawal.

Prevalence of cannabis dependence

Poulton *et al.* (1997) examined cannabis dependence among the Dunedin Multidisciplinary Health and Development Study (DMHDS) cohort. At the ages of 18 and 21 years, participants were asked a series of questions based on the DSM-III-R criteria for substance dependence (APA 1987). The rate of cannabis dependence among 18-year-olds was 6.6% and rose to 9.6% by the age of 21. At age 18, approximately twice as many males than females were dependent on the drug. While the rate of dependence increased only marginally for females between ages 18 (4.4%) and 21 (4.7%), it rose sharply from 8.6% to 14.3% among males. Of those diagnosed dependent at age 18, approximately half remained cannabis dependent at age 21.

Similar estimates of dependence in young adulthood were found among the cohort of the Christchurch Health and Development Study (CHDS) (Fergusson and Horwood 2000a; Fergusson *et al.* 2003b). At age 17, 3.6% of the sample met the DSM-IV criteria for cannabis dependence (APA 1994). By the age of 21, the proportion had increased to 9%, with rates significantly higher among males (13.1%) than females (5%). Among the 198 participants who had used cannabis prior to the age of 16, the rate of dependence at age 21 was 21.7%. Almost all (95%) of those classified as cannabis dependent reported using the drug more than once a week for a period of at least one year. These respondents reported using the drug an average of 320 times between the ages of 16 and 21.

However, much lower rates of cannabis dependence were recorded among the sample of 14- to 17 year-olds from the Early Developmental Stages of Psychopathology Study (EDSPS) in Munich, Germany (Perkonigg *et al.* 1999). Only six of the 1228 adolescents who participated in the baseline assessment met the DSM-IV criteria for cannabis dependence (APA 1994), with a further six cases during the period to the follow-up assessment.

The 1998 National Household Survey on Drug Abuse (NHSDA), a continuing cross-sectional survey of US citizens aged 12 and older, found that among respondents using marijuana during the last year, 27% of 12- to 17-year-olds had three or more dependence problems compared with 15% of adults (US SAMHSA 2000). To address the possibility of an age-related bias in the reporting of dependence, Chen and Anthony (2003) analysed data from the 1995–98 NHSDA dataset, involving a total of 1866 adolescents and 762 adults. All were classified as recent-onset marijuana users (i.e. users of the drug for the first time during the previous year), so as to control for the possibility of 'period effects' resulting from the exposure of younger users to higher concentrations of delta-9-tetra hydrocannabinol (THC) than those found in previous years (ElSohly *et al.* 2000). After controlling for the effects of variables such as sex, race, ethnicity, the cumulative number of days of marijuana use since first using the drug, and a history of alcohol or other drug use, adolescent recent-onset users were found to be more likely than adults to report clinical features of marijuana dependence. For example, they were two times more likely than adult users to report being unable to cut down on their marijuana use and 2.6 times more likely to report health problems as a result of using the drug. Following statistical analyses that held the underlying level of marijuana dependence in the two age groups constant, adolescents were still more likely than adults to report two features of dependence, namely tolerance of the drug's effects and being unable to cut down on their use of the drug. Chen and Anthony (2003) suggested that this might reflect differences in the phenomenological meaning of concepts such as 'being unable to cut down' between adolescents and adult users.

Cannabis potency

Much of the recent media attention on cannabis in the UK has focused on the strength of different forms of the drug, most notably 'skunk' (BBC 2005b). The European Monitoring Centre for Drugs and Drug Addiction (EMCDDA) has published a report examining the evidence on recent trends in cannabis potency across the continent (EMCDDA 2004a). Information was collected from a review of the published and unpublished 'grey' literature and responses to a questionnaire sent to 26 European countries via the Reitox focal points, which collect drug-related information for the EMCDDA. The report concluded that although there have been increases in cannabis potency (i.e. THC content) in some countries, these changes are largely attributable to intensively grown domestic products. Overall, 'effective' potency levels, taking into account the relative consumption of different cannabis products in different countries, have remained at around 6 to 8% in Austria, the Czech Republic, Germany, Portugal and the UK for a number of years. The sole exception is the Netherlands, where home grown products account for over half of the cannabis used. For most countries, imported cannabis constitutes the bulk of consumption, and there has been no marked upward trend in the strength of these products.

Summary

The latest findings of the Health Behaviour in School-aged Children study (HBSC), which includes samples from Europe and North America, show that among 15-year-olds, around a fifth of females and a quarter of males have tried cannabis at least once in their lives. Around 3% are classified as 'heavy' users of the drug (40 or more times). However, there is considerable variation between countries in the levels of both 'lifetime' and more recent use, with over 30% of pupils in England, Canada, Greenland, Scotland, Spain, Switzerland and the US reporting use of the drug in the past year.

Recent surveys conducted in the UK have found that the proportion of school pupils who have used the drug increases sharply from the age of 13 onwards, with over a quarter reporting past-year use by the age of 15. There is some evidence of higher prevalence among students who describe their ethnic status as 'Black', but national surveys are generally lacking in detailed figures of substance use among different ethnic groups. Cannabis use is higher among pupils who have been suspended or expelled from school. Around a quarter of older adolescents (aged 16 and over) report using the drug during the last year, although figures are much higher among the young homeless and young offenders.

A number of large-scale, longitudinal cohort studies in Australia, Germany and New Zealand have provided information on changes in the patterns of cannabis use during the course of adolescence. The general pattern of findings indicates that while most younger adolescents who have never tried the drug remain non-users during the teenage years, a majority of early users continue at some level of use throughout adolescence. Two recent studies have conducted analyses of cannabis data to identify discrete trajectories of use over time.

Cohort studies conducted in New Zealand have found rates of cannabis dependence of around 4% among 18-year-olds, increasing to around 9% at age 21, with higher prevalence among males and those who had used the drug before the age of 16. However, considerably lower levels of dependence were reported in a cohort study in Germany. There is some debate over whether withdrawal symptoms, one of the criteria used to determine substance dependence, have any clinical significicance in the case of cannabis. The pattern, onset, duration and abatement of symptoms among former cannabis users are inconsistent.

Contrary to recent media reports over the strength of cannabis products currently in use, a recent report by the European Monitoring Centre for Drugs and Drug Addiction (EMCDDA) has concluded that overall levels of the drug's potency have remained fairly stable in recent years. The increases that have been recorded are confined largely to intensively cultivated domestic products, rather than imported supplies, which constitute the bulk of consumption in most countries.

3 Young People's Views about Cannabis

Perceptions of harm

A number of studies examining attitudes to drug use among children and adolescents have noted that cannabis is often viewed quite differently from other illicit substances. McIntosh, MacDonald and McKeganey (2003) surveyed a sample of over 2000 10- to 12-year-olds at 47 schools in Glasgow and Newcastle-Upon-Tyne, UK. All the pupils present at the schools on the days of the survey were asked to complete a questionnaire about their attitudes towards and experiences of illegal drugs. A sub-sample of 230 children was then invited to take part in semi-structured interviews to obtain further details on these topics. Of the 216 who agreed to be interviewed, 43 had used drugs at least once before, 42 had been offered but not used them, and 131 had neither been offered nor used. Around a quarter of those interviewed regarded all illegal drugs in a negative way, but the remainder were able to discriminate between different substances in terms of their perceived harmful effects. While heroin, ecstasy and cocaine were seen as having the most serious consequences, cannabis was often viewed as a relatively benign drug (e.g. similar to smoking but 'stronger'), no more harmful than alcohol or tobacco, and having a number of positive features (e.g. getting high, a way of forgetting problems, improving mood and aiding sleep). A number of negative consequences were noted, however, including the potential impact of smoking on physical fitness, encouraging the use of other illicit drugs, and certain aspects of being under the drug's influence (e.g. apathy, talking nonsense, increased appetite).

Pearson and Shiner (2002) reported on the findings from two public opinion surveys in the UK commissioned by the Independent Inquiry into the Misuse of Drugs Act (Police Foundation 2000). One of the surveys involved a sample of over 3500 11- to 16-year-olds (MORI Social Research 1999). Respondents were asked to rate alcohol, tobacco and a range of illicit drugs according to their perceived harmful effects ('very harmful', 'fairly harmful', 'not very harmful' or 'not at all harmful'). Over 90% of 11- and 12-year-olds regarded all illicit drugs, including cannabis, as either 'very' or 'fairly harmful', although alcohol and tobacco were seen as much less harmful. However, by the ages of 15 and 16, a majority of the respondents no longer viewed cannabis in this way, while perceptions of harm for ecstasy, heroin, cocaine and amphetamine remained at their previous high level.

The study by Wibberley and Price (2000) featured a sample of pupils, aged 15 to 16 years, from nine schools in and around Greater Manchester, UK. A total of 1067 questionnaires detailing pupils' feelings about drug use were completed during lesson time. One of the items asked pupils to rate how risky they thought the taking of various drugs might be in terms of their health. Cannabis was rated as 'low risk', 'very low risk' or 'no risk' by just over two-thirds (67.3%) of respondents, compared with 24.8% in the case of amphetamine and 1.3% for heroin. Of those who had ever used cannabis, 85.7% rated the drug in this manner, compared with 53.6% of those who had never tried the drug.

Attitudes toward peer use

The Greater Manchester study (Wibberley and Price 2000) also asked pupils how true they thought certain statements would be if a close friend of theirs were to use various drugs. For the statement 'It wouldn't bother me, because I don't see anything wrong with it', 51.3% considered this to be either 'true' or 'very true' if the drug was cannabis, compared with 24.8% for amphetamine and 3.6% for heroin. Pupils who had already used that particular drug were more likely to endorse the statement than non-users. In the case of cannabis, 75.6% of those who had ever used the drug would not be bothered by a friend's use, compared with 26.1% of non-users. Similar patterns were found in response to the statement 'It wouldn't bother me, it's their choice, nothing to do with me', with 67.7%

rating this as 'true' or 'very 'true' in the case of cannabis, 37.6% for amphetamine and 18.7% for heroin. However, respondents were less likely to endorse the statement 'It would worry me, and I'd talk to them to try and stop them using it' if the drug were cannabis (41%), compared with 65.4% in the case of amphetamine and 81% for heroin.

Perceived functions of use

A number of studies have examined the reasons that young people give for using drugs in terms of a 'functional' perspective – that is, the primary purpose served by the use of a particular substance (Boys *et al.* 1999; Boys and Marsden 2003; Boys, Marsden and Strang 2001). Boys *et al.* (2001) assessed the perceived functions of cannabis and five other substances (alcohol, amphetamine, cocaine, ecstasy and lysergic acid diethylamide [LSD]) among a sample of 364 16- to 22-year-olds in the UK. They were recruited using a snowballing approach, whereby a team of peer interviewers was trained to recruit and interview participants. All participants had used two or more illegal substances during the 90 days prior to the interview but had no history of treatment for substance-related disorders. Data were collected using a structured interviewer-administered questionnaire, which included a 17-item scale measuring the perceived functions of using each of the six listed drugs. These included changing mood (e.g. 'make yourself feel better when down or depressed'), physical effects (e.g. 'help you to sleep'), social purpose (e.g. 'help you enjoy the company of friends'), facilitating activity (e.g. 'enhance an activity such as listening to music or playing a game or sport') and managing effects from other substances (e.g. 'help ease the after-effects of other substances'). Participants were asked if they had ever used a particular drug for each of the listed functions and, if so, how often they had done so over the past year.

Boys *et al.* (2001) noted that among participants who had used cannabis over the past year, the two most popular functions for using the drug were to 'help you to relax' (96.8%) and 'just get really stoned or intoxicated' (90.7%). Over two-thirds of this group also used cannabis to 'enhance an activity such as listening to music or playing a game or sport' (72.8%), 'help make something you were doing less boring' (70.1%), 'help you to sleep' (69.6%), and 'make yourself feel better when down or depressed' (69.0%). Male participants were more likely than females to say that they had used cannabis to 'help you keep going on a night out with friends' in the past year. Participants who had used cannabis to 'help you feel elated or euphoric' or to 'help you to sleep' were significantly older than those who had not used cannabis for these purposes. Those who had used cannabis to 'help you feel more confident or more able to talk to people in a social situation' and to 'help you stop worrying about a problem' were younger than those who had not used the drug for these reasons.

Boys *et al.* (1999) have documented significant relationships between perceived functions and both the recent use of a particular drug and intentions to use the drug again in the future. Data were collected from a cross-sectional survey of 100 young people, aged between 16 and 21 years, from Southern England. Snowballing techniques were again employed to recruit participants. In addition to answering questions on the perceived functions of their drug use, respondents reported the frequency of their recent use (the total number of days drugs were used in the previous 90 days) and the likelihood of using the drug again in the next 12 months. A total of 67 respondents reported recent use of cannabis. Higher scores on a three-item 'mood function' scale (e.g. using the drug to 'make yourself better when you were low or depressed') were associated with more frequent use and a greater intensity of cannabis use in the three months prior to interview. Higher scores on a five-item 'social/contextual function' scale (e.g. using the drug to 'help you to feel more confident in a social situation') were associated with a greater frequency, though not intensity, of recent cannabis use. Higher scores on both the mood function and social/contextual function scales also predicted greater intentions to use cannabis in the next 12 months.

Perceived functions of drug use are also associated with the level of drug-related problems. The study by Boys and Marsden (2003) involved the same sample of 364 young people featured in an earlier paper (Boys *et al.* 2001). A selection of items from the tenth edition of the International Statistical Classification of Diseases and Related Health Problems (ICD-10) (World Health Organization 1992) and DSM-IV (APA 1994) were used to assess recent (i.e. past-year) drug-related problems, including preoccupation, worry or concern, social problems, prioritising spending money on drug use, role neglect, regretting actions while intoxicated and loss of control. A total of 344 participants reported using cannabis in the 90 days prior to the interview. Higher scores on a three-item 'negative mood' function subscale (e.g. using the drug to 'help stop worrying about a problem') and using the drug to 'feel elated or euphoric' were associated with more reports of cannabis-related problems during the past year.

The social context of use

A study by Bell *et al.* (1998) has noted that changes in the way young people view and use cannabis often mirror events occurring in other areas of their lives. Participants were 15-year-old males who were recruited from two state comprehensive schools on the east coast of Scotland and interviewed three times over a period of 18 months. At the first round of interviews, 106 individuals took part, representing around a third of all secondary year 4 pupils in both schools. A questionnaire was used to collect socio-demographic characteristics of the sample and information on education, work, leisure activities and health-related behaviours. This was followed by a semi-structured interview, covering the questionnaire topics in greater detail. To illustrate the changes occurring in the partici- pants' lives over the 18-month period, Bell *et al.* (1998) used a case study approach and reported the findings from the three rounds of interviews conducted with three participants ('John', 'Mark' and 'Jamie').

At the first interview, 'John' reported that he drank alcohol regularly but had never smoked tobacco and, although not referring specifically to cannabis, held negative views about illicit drugs (e.g. they are bad for your health and used by people who get into trouble with the police). His social life involved meeting friends either on the streets or at the local community centre. 'John' commented that because he did not mix with peers who used drugs, he had never had the opportunity to try them. However, by the third interview at the age of 17, he had begun to use cannabis at least once a week. A number of events had occurred in the previous year, including missing the application deadline for entry into college and splitting up with his girlfriend. 'John' had started socialising again with his former school friends, some of whom were now using cannabis.

When first interviewed, 'Mark' said that he had had no direct contact with illicit drugs. By the time of the second interview eight months later, he had become an occasional user of cannabis, which he attributed, in part, to an earlier decision to socialise more after a period of working too hard at school. By the third interview, however, he had all but given up using cannabis and was critical of his earlier experiences of the drug (e.g. a waste of money and having no real benefits).

The third case study, 'Jamie', reported using cannabis several times a week at the time of the first interview and had also tried amphetamines and LSD. His use of drugs and alcohol was partly for recreational reasons but also as a means of coping with personal problems, such as splitting up with his girlfriend and the death of his grandmother. At the second interview, by which time he had left school and started work, he gave some indication of wanting to cut down on his cannabis use on the grounds that he would have to sooner or later if he were to get married and have children. However, he noted the difficulty in attempting to stop using cannabis while his friends continued to use it. By the third interview, he had restricted his cannabis use to the weekends only and explained this new pattern in terms of wanting to 'feel fresh' for his new job.

The influence of gender roles

Warner, Weber and Albanes (1999) examined the ways in which gender roles influence adolescents in their use of marijuana. The study comprised 42 focus groups involving 122 male and 110 female participants from nine high schools in Ontario, Canada. In each focus group, participants were asked whether there were any differences in how males and females used marijuana, where and when each group used it, and how each group went about obtaining the drug.

While the need to 'fit in' was cited as a reason for marijuana use among males, the need to 'be pretty' was identified as a constraint on females' use, together with concerns about the drug's potential to cause premature ageing. Males were considered to have a rather blasé attitude to the possible health consequences of marijuana. An additional constraint on females' use of marijuana was the tendency for peers to view such behaviour as 'deviant', while generally accepting males' use of the drug.

Most participants said that females were more careful in choosing where and when they used marijuana. Males were more likely to use the drug in public, while females tended to use it in more private settings to reduce the risk of detection and possible punishment. However, females would sometimes smoke marijuana with a group of males as a means of gaining social acceptance.

Very few of the female participants in the focus groups stated that they themselves or their female friends had ever purchased marijuana directly from a dealer. They stated that this was because most dealers were male, who were seen as being more likely to cheat or harass female customers than male ones. Females usually obtained supplies of marijuana from male intermediaries, who either shared their own supplies or acted as brokers with male dealers.

One way in which females dealt with the variety of obstacles limiting their access to marijuana was to claim moral, intellectual or developmental superiority over male peers. For example, some female participants felt that, unlike males, they were able to achieve greater intimacy with their friends without having to resort to marijuana to become less inhibited.

Cannabis and tobacco

A number of studies have examined the relationship between the use of cannabis and tobacco among adolescents. Amos *et al.* (2004) reported on two qualitative studies of smokers (defined as having smoked at least one cigarette in the preceding week) in the Lothian region of Scotland. The first study involved 46 15- to 16-year-old smokers who participated in focus groups, and the second study featured paired interviews with 99 16- to 19-year-old smokers. Although the primary purpose of both studies was to examine smoking behaviours, the focus group and paired interviews revealed that cannabis use was an important part of many participants' lives and linked to cigarette smoking in a number of ways.

Most participants had begun smoking cigarettes before using cannabis, but a few had tried the drug first. Among these individuals, smoking cannabis in combination with tobacco in the form of joints had led them to start smoking normal cigarettes. This occurred as a result of becoming used to or addicted to the tobacco content of the joint and smoking cigarettes when they either had no cannabis or were unable to use it – for example, when they were at school. For many regular cannabis users, consuming cannabis in the form of joints served to reinforce their tobacco use. Most participants had tried to stop cigarette smoking but had found this difficult, due in part to their continued use of cannabis. Few cannabis users intended to stop using the drug because of its positive aspects, such as relieving stress and enhancing mood.

Similar findings concerning the role of cannabis in supporting cigarette smoking were reported by Highet (2004) in a sample of 59 13- to 15-year-olds recruited from youth clubs in the Lothian region. This study also documented differences in the ways that the teenagers regarded cannabis and tobacco. Cigarettes were seen primarily in terms of their addictive potential, while cannabis simply gets you 'high', does not lead to dependence and may counteract the harm caused by cigarettes by 'diluting' the smoke from tobacco.

Reasons for not using cannabis

Relatively little research has been conducted into young people's reasons for not using cannabis. Fountain *et al.* (1999) documented reasons for the non-use of licit and illicit drugs among a sample of 100 young people, aged 13 to 22 years, who were recruited from a variety of settings (e.g. youth club, school sixth form, drug awareness outreach project) in the Greater London area. Eighteen individuals stated that they had never used cannabis. Being uninterested in the effects of cannabis was the most common reason given for not using the drug (6 out of 18). Four respondents said it was because they were afraid of the effects. Other reasons, cited by a single respondent in each case, were fear of addiction, lack of opportunity for use and witnessing the effect of cannabis on others.

Rogers and McCarthy (1999) conducted an interview-based study of 158 12- to 13-year-olds from 18 schools in the London boroughs of Camden and Islington. Nine pupils stated that they used cannabis in the past, although only two reported current use. The most common reason for not using, or no longer using, drugs in general centred around the harmful effects on health. Additional reasons given by the participants were the possibility of becoming addicted, getting into trouble at school or with parents or the police, the cost of buying the drug, not having the opportunity of using it, and having better things to do with their time and money.

Summary

A number of studies examining attitudes to drug use among children and adolescents have noted that cannabis is often viewed quite differently from other illicit substances. Cannabis tends to be seen as posing less of a risk to health than 'hard' drugs such as amphetamines or heroin, and no more harmful than alcohol or tobacco. Adolescents are also less concerned about the use of cannabis by their friends than other drugs.

Studies based on a 'functional' perspective of substance use have found that cannabis is used for a variety of reasons, including relaxation, intoxication, enhancement of leisure activities such as listening to music, aiding sleep and lifting mood. The perceived functions of cannabis use are also associated with intentions to use the drug in the future, the frequency and intensity of this use, and the level of drug-related problems.

Changes in the way that young people regard and use cannabis are often mirrored by events occurring in other areas of their lives. Cannabis use may develop as a means of coping with particular problems and it may be encouraged by the use of the drug among the individual's peer group. Gender also has an influence, with the need to fit in and be accepted as contributory factors in the case of males, while concerns over physical appearance, the possible health effects of the drug and peer disapproval over drug-taking can act as a constraint on females' use.

Cannabis and tobacco are often viewed by adolescents as being closely linked in a number of ways. The smoking of cannabis in combination with tobacco in the form of joints is cited by some as a reason for starting to smoke 'normal' cigarettes, reinforcing their subsequent use and making it difficult to stop smoking in the future.

Relatively little research has looked into the reasons for not using cannabis. Among the reasons cited for non-use are being uninterested in the effects of the drug, its potentially harmful effects on health, the possibility of becoming addicted, getting into trouble at school or with parents or the police, the cost of buying the drug and not having the opportunity to use it.

4 Predictors of Cannabis Use

The identification of variables that predict the future use of cannabis among adolescents is important as it can enable the more effective targeting of prevention strategies. Longitudinal studies in Australia, New Zealand, Norway and the US have provided a wealth of information on variables that predict the various stages of cannabis use, including first-time use, continued and regular use, the development of cannabis dependence and the likelihood of stopping use.

Initiation of use

Predictors of first-time cannabis use were examined by Coffey *et al.* (2000) among a sample of school pupils from the Victorian Adolescent Health Cohort Study in Australia. Data were collected at six assessment points or waves, with participants completing a questionnaire at six-month intervals, beginning at the ages of 14 to 15 years (school year 9). For the purposes of the data analyses, cannabis use was summarised in terms of the highest level of use occurring over two periods of the study: 'mid-school' (waves 2 and 3) and 'late-school' (waves 4 to 6). A range of demographic, social, peer and individual factors measured in the mid-school period were examined as possible predictors of cannabis use during late-school.

A total of 1347 pupils were identified as first-time users of cannabis (at least one episode of use during the late-school period with no use in mid-school). Daily smoking, frequent and high-dose alcohol use (i.e three or more days in the previous week and an average of five units or more per drinking day), antisocial behaviours (e.g. property damage, interpersonal conflict, theft) and the use of cannabis by peers were all significant predictors of the initiation of cannabis use in the late-school period. A high level of school cannabis use in mid-school (defined as the proportion of students within each school using the drug at least weekly) was also associated with an increased likelihood of first-time cannabis use during late-school.

Van den Bree and Pickworth (2005) reported the findings from a sample of middle and high school students, aged 11 to 21 years, who were participating in the National Longitudinal Study of Adolescent Health (Add Health) in the US. Over 16,000 individuals from 134 schools were randomly selected to take part in interviews conducted at home, with data collected at two time points one year apart. At the first assessment, participants reported how many times they had used marijuana during their lives and were also assessed on a total of 21 potential predictor variables. These included daily activities, psychological health, personality, school situation (e.g. trouble at school, dissatisfaction with school), family functioning, 'rough living' (e.g. involvement with other substances such as alcohol and tobacco, delinquency), religion and neighbourhood (e.g. looking out for others, knowing most neighbours). At the second assessment, participants reported on their use of the drug during the previous year.

The initiation of experimental use (one to ten times) or regular use (more than ten times) of marijuana was examined by selecting non-users at the first assessment and comparing those who reported use by the second assessment with those who remained non-users. After controlling for the effects of age, race, and urban and socio-economic status, the analyses showed that involvement with other substances, peer use of other substances, and delinquency were significant predictors of first-time experimental marijuana use. Being in trouble in school (e.g. trouble with teachers, skipping school, being expelled) was also a predictor for male participants, while being unhappy in school and reporting low religiosity were additional predictors for females. For the initiation of regular marijuana use, involvement with other substances, trouble in school, delinquency and low religiosity were all significant predictors.

Conduct problems and attention deficit behaviours have been the focus of a number of studies examining predictors of adolescent cannabis use. Fergusson, Lynskey and Horwood (1993) studied the relationship between these behaviours measured during childhood and cannabis use at the age of 15. The data were collected from the birth cohort of the Christchurch Health and Development Study. Problem behaviours were measured using a combination of maternal and teacher reports at the ages of 6, 8 and 12 years, while adolescent cannabis use was assessed by self and parental reports. Analyses were performed on data from 875 participants (69.2% of the original cohort) for whom complete data were available on all the variables. Although high conduct problem scores at all four ages in childhood were associated with an increased risk of using cannabis at age 15, attention deficit behaviours were not significantly related to later cannabis use after their relationship with conduct problems was taken into account. The association between conduct problems and cannabis use remained significant after controlling for a series of potentially confounding factors, including family social position, family living standards and parental discord. Children with high conduct problem scores had risks of later cannabis use that were between 2.1 and 2.7 times higher than children with low scores.

Pedersen, Mastekaasa and Wichstrom (2001) investigated the associations between different types of conduct problem and later cannabis use among a sample of 2436 adolescents in Norway. Students in the seventh and eighth grades of high school (ages 13 to 14) completed a self-administered questionnaire and were followed up a year and a half later. Three types of conduct problem were measured: 'serious' (stealing or vandalism), 'aggressive' (e.g. violent quarrel with or cursing in front of a teacher) and 'covert' (e.g. getting onto a bus without paying, playing truant).

A total of 99 students had used cannabis for the first time by the follow-up assessment. Less than 1% of individuals who reported no conduct problems at the baseline assessment had used cannabis by the follow-up, compared with 34.5% of those with eight or more problems. After controlling for a number of potentially confounding social, family and peer-related variables, there was a significant association between early conduct problems and later cannabis initiation, with a stronger relationship in the case of females. For the different types of conduct problem, there were a number of gender differences in the observed associations with cannabis use. The 'serious' category of conduct problems showed a significant relationship with later cannabis use for males but not for females. Levels of both 'aggressive' and 'covert' behaviours, however, were associated with the initiation of cannabis use for females but not males by the time of follow-up.

Developmental variations in initiation

There is some evidence of a shift in the relative influence of parental and peer-related factors on marijuana use as adolescents get older. Bailey and Hubbard (1990) analysed data from a sample of 3454 secondary school students who were taking part in a large substance abuse prevention study in southeastern US. Participants completed a self-administered question-naire and were followed up a year later. The effects of three sets of vari-ables on marijuana initiation were examined: social control (e.g. attach-ment to parents, peers and school), social learning (e.g. the attitudes of parents and peers towards drugs and the use of drugs by the peer group), and the expected costs and benefits of marijuana use. Results were compared for students in three groups: sixth/seventh, seventh/eighth and eighth/ninth grades.

The proportion of students reporting first-time marijuana use during the follow-up period was 9.7% for the sixth/seventh grades, 13.9% for the seventh/eighth grades, and 18.7% for the eighth/ninth grades. Only parental attachment measures were significantly related to later marijuana initiation among the sixth/seventh-grade students. It was originally pre-dicted that adolescents with higher levels of parental attachment, as indi-cated by the importance of and ability to communicate with their parents, would be less likely to try marijuana. Although a greater perceived importance of communicating with parents was associated with a lower likelihood of initiation, a greater perceived ability to communicate was related to an increased likelihood of marijuana use. This latter finding was interpreted by the study's authors as indicating either a liberal attitude towards drug taking on the part of parents or a degree of preco-ciousness on the part of the students. In the case of the middle age group (seventh/eighth grades), however, a combination of parental and peer attachment measures, together with peer exposure variables, predicted first-time use of marijuana. A greater perceived importance of communi-cation and a greater ability to communicate with parents were both associated with a lower likelihood of initiation. A higher level of communication with peers was related to a greater likelihood of initiation, but greater disapproval of alcohol and drug use by peers was related to a decreased likelihood of initiation. For the oldest age group (eighth/ninth grades), none of the parental attachment variables were significantly associated with marijuana initiation. However, measures of peer attachment, attitude and behaviour, together with the relative importance of the costs of marijuana use (i.e. negative consequences), predicted initiation for these students. Those who believed that the costs of using marijuana were relatively unimportant and whose peer group both approved of and used marijuana or alcohol were more likely to begin using the drug during the year to follow-up.

The study by Ellickson *et al.* (2004b) featured a cohort of 1995 seventh- to tenth-grade students from 30 schools in the states of California and Oregon, US, who were taking part in the RAND Adolescent/Young Adult Panel Study. Students completed self-administered surveys assessing their lifetime use of marijuana and a range of predictor variables. These included problem behaviours (e.g. delinquency), social influences on marijuana use (e.g. peer use), and marijuana-related attitudes and behaviour (e.g. perceived harmfulness). Predictors of first-time use during the one-year follow-up were analysed for participants in the seventh, eighth and ninth grades.

Across all grades, the initiation of marijuana use was predicted by more frequent cigarette use, more frequent marijuana offers and poor academic grades, after controlling for the effects of all other variables. However, there were some differences between the grades in terms of the influence of particular variables. Among seventh-grade students, more frequent alcohol use, more frequent intentions to use marijuana in the next six months, less parental education, lack of communication with parents and greater rebelliousness were additional predictors of marijuana initiation one year later. Additional significant predictors of first-time use among grade 8 students were marijuana use by older siblings, low marijuana resistance self-efficacy (i.e. the ability to refuse an offer of marijuana), and weaker beliefs in the harmful effects of marijuana. In the case of ninth-grade students, more frequent alcohol use and greater peer approval of marijuana use were also associated with a greater likelihood of marijuana use during the one-year follow-up.

Using data from the Add Health study in the US, van den Bree and Pickworth (2005) divided the sample of over 13,000 students into two age groups (11 to 15 years and 16 to 21 years) to assess differences in the impact of particular predictor variables. For the initiation of experimental marijuana use (one to ten times) during the one year to follow-up, four variables were significant predictors among female students in the 11 to 15 age group: own and peer involvement with other substances, delinquency, unhappiness in school and low religiosity. In the older group, however, only own and peer involvement with substances and low religiosity remained significant predictors. For the initiation of regular use (more than ten times), own and peer involvement with substances and trouble in school were significant predictors for both genders in both age groups. Delinquency and irrational decision making (e.g. not seeing many approaches to problems, not researching solutions) were additional predictors of initiation among 11- to 15-year-olds, while engaging in 'inactive' pastimes (e.g. watching television, playing computer games) was also a predictor for 16- to 21-year-olds.

Continued and regular use

Bailey, Flewelling and Rachal (1992) examined the determinants of continued marijuana use in adolescence, focusing in particular on the relative influence of social context and drug-specific factors. The study analysed data from a sample of secondary and high school students in southeastern US who had already experimented with marijuana (i.e. used one to five times). Potential predictors of continued use at follow-up approximately two years later were grouped into two main categories. Social context predictors included friends' use of marijuana, availability of the drug and the attitudes of friends and parents to drug use. Examples of drug-specific predictors were the reporting of 'getting high' or 'stoned' when smoking marijuana, trying the drug out of curiosity and beliefs about the physical or psychological risks related to taking the drug.

Of the 456 students who had reported marijuana use at the initial assessment, 37.9% were classified as continued users (i.e. used the drug six or more times) by the time of the follow-up. The analyses showed that only drug-specific factors were significantly associated with continued use of marijuana. Students who reported getting stoned were nearly two times more likely than those who did not experience this effect to continue using marijuana. Those who felt that the adverse effects of marijuana use (e.g. using marijuana can hurt my health, it can make me feel depressed, marijuana is addictive) were unimportant reasons for not using the drug were the most likely to continue using. None of the social context measures were significant predictors of continued use.

Analysing data from the Victorian Adolescent Health Cohort Study, Coffey *et al.* (2000) classified a total of 283 students reporting any level of use in both the 'mid-school' (waves 2 and 3 of data collection) and 'late-school' (waves 4 to 6) periods of the study as continued users. Students who were occasional smokers (defined as smoking during the last month but less than six days in the previous week) during mid-school were two times more likely than non-smokers to continue marijuana use during late-school, and daily smokers were over three times more likely. More frequent cannabis use (once a week or more) and use of the drug by peers during mid-school were also significantly associated with an increased risk of continued use.

Van den Bree and Pickworth (2005) examined predictors of the progression to regular use of marijuana (more than ten times) among the sample of 11- to 21-year-olds from the Add Health study in the US. Delinquency and independent decision-making (e.g. making choices about amount and type of television programmes watched, clothing and diet) were significant predictors of regular use among male students, while trouble in school was a significant predictor for females.

Dependence

Adolescent predictors of cannabis dependence in young adulthood were examined by Coffey *et al.* (2003), involving 1601 participants from the Victorian Adolescent Health Cohort Study. Dependence was assessed at ages 20 to 21 years according to DSM-IV criteria (APA 1994). Potential predictors of dependence were measured at six assessment points during the school years (years 9 to 12) and included cannabis use, cigarette smoking, alcohol consumption, antisocial behaviour and psychiatric morbidity. Responses on these measures were summarised in terms of the number of assessment points or waves at which they were given. For example, the reporting of alcohol consumption at four or more waves indicated 'persistent' exposure to this factor.

A total of 115 participants at age 21 (7% of those providing data at this assessment) met the diagnostic criteria for cannabis dependence during the previous year. Dependence was more likely among participants who were male and reported weekly or daily cannabis use, persistent cigarette smoking and persistent antisocial behaviour during their school years. The analyses also found a significant interaction between alcohol consumption and weekly or daily cannabis use, such that cannabis use was no longer associated with an increased risk of later dependence for participants who reported frequent drinking (i.e. measured at two or more waves). This latter finding was interpreted by the study's authors as indicating a process whereby individuals opt for either a predominantly alcohol- or cannabis-using lifestyle.

Fergusson and Horwood (2000a) analysed the relationships between a variety of social, family and childhood variables measured at age 15 and cannabis dependence at the age of 21 in the cohort of the Christchurch Health and Development Study. The significant predictors of dependence, defined according to DSM-IV criteria (APA 1994), were male gender, deviant peer affiliations, novelty seeking and conduct problems. A later analysis of the same cohort (Fergusson *et al.* 2003b) examined the extent to which responses to early cannabis use were associated with subsequent cannabis dependence at age 21. At the ages of 15 and 16 years, participants were interviewed about their use of cannabis in the previous 12 months. Those who reported using the drug were asked to report their subjective reactions on the last or most recent occasion of use based on a series of eight items that described positive experiences (e.g. got really high, felt happy) and negative ones (e.g. felt ill/dizzy, passed out).

Of the 1011 participants questioned at age 21, 198 had used cannabis prior to the age of 16 years, with 21.7% meeting the criteria for cannabis dependence. Early positive reactions to cannabis at the ages of 14 to 16 were associated with significantly increased risks of dependence during the period from 16 to 21. For example, 34.1% of participants who stated that they 'got really high' met the criteria for dependence, compared with 12.4% of those who did not report this reaction. Statistical adjustment for potential confounding factors, such as the frequency of cannabis use before the age of 16 and a range of family and social variables, had little effect on the strength of the association between early positive reactions and later dependence. Dependence was unrelated to early negative reactions to the drug, although the authors of the study acknowledged that this might have been due to the fact that these experiences were relatively uncommon among the sample.

Cessation of use

A study by Sussmann and Dent (1999) examined predictors of marijuana use cessation among a cohort of adolescents from 21 continuation high schools (i.e. students who have been transferred out of the regular school system due to functional problems such as drug use) in the US. At the baseline assessment, 54% of the 566 students, aged 14 to 19 years, reported using marijuana in the previous month. A total of 40 social, attitude, intrapersonal, violence-related, drug-use-related and demographic variables were measured as potential predictors of marijuana cessation or 'quit' status a year later. Quitting was defined as having not used marijuana in the 30 days prior to the follow-up assessment and having no intention to use the drug in the future. At follow-up, 31% of the baseline marijuana users were classified as achieving quit status. After controlling for covariation among the variables, the significant predictors of quit status were age, the extent of peer approval of marijuana use, feelings about the morality of drug use, and victimisation. Individuals who, at the time of the baseline assessment, were older and reported receiving less approval from their peers for using drugs, held unfavourable attitudes about the acceptability of drug use, reported less victimisation in the last year and were more likely to have stopped using the drug by the follow-up.

Sussman and Dent (2004) extended their analysis of marijuana use cessation in this cohort over five years into young adulthood. The study featured the previous set of 40 predictor variables with some additional variables relating to young adults' social roles, such as employment, marital and parental status. At the five-year follow-up, 42% of baseline marijuana users had stopped using the drug. After controlling for covariation among the variables, gender, baseline level of marijuana use and young adult marital status were found to be significant predictors of quit status. Female participants and those who reported lower marijuana use and a conventional adult social role at baseline were more likely to have stopped using marijuana by the follow-up.

Summary

A number of large-scale, longitudinal cohort studies have examined the predictors of various stages of cannabis use during adolescence, including first-time use, the progression to continued and/or regular use, the development of cannabis dependence and the likelihood of stopping use.

The initiation of cannabis use is predicted by a range of factors. These include the use of other substances (e.g. daily smoking and frequent and high levels of alcohol use), the use of cannabis and other drugs by the individual's peer group, a high level of cannabis use in school, school-related problems (e.g. trouble with teachers, truanting from school, being expelled, unhappy at school), antisocial behaviours, low religiosity and conduct problems in childhood. There is some evidence of a shift in the relative influence of parental and peer-related factors on the use of cannabis as adolescents get older. For example, the perceived importance of and ability to communicate with parents appears to exert a greater impact on the initiation of cannabis use among younger adolescents. For older adolescents, first-time use is influenced more by the attitudes and behaviours of the peer group, together with individual beliefs about the effects of cannabis and the ability to refuse offers of the drug.

Many of the factors that predict first-time use also contribute to the continued use of cannabis and the development of dependence. Both of these patterns of use are predicted by higher frequency cannabis use earlier in adolescence. The risk of later dependence is also associated with earlier positive reactions to using the drug.

The cessation of cannabis use in late adolescence and young adulthood is more likely among female users, and those who reported lower use of the drug earlier in adolescence, received less approval from peers for using drugs, held more negative attitudes to drug use, and had assumed a conventional adult social role, such as marriage.

5 Cannabis and Psychosocial Functioning

Much of the recent media attention on cannabis has focused on its potential role in the development of psychotic illness. A number of national surveys have found that rates of cannabis use among people with schizophrenia are approximately twice as high as those in the general population (Hall and Degenhardt 2000; Regier, Farmer and Rae 1990; Robins and Regier 1991; Tien and Anthony 1990; van Os *et al.* 2002). However, cannabis use is also linked to a range of other psychosocial outcomes. For example, a 1999 survey of child and adolescent mental health in the UK revealed that, among 13- to 15-year-olds, those who had used cannabis were nearly two times more likely than non-users to be diagnosed with a depressive disorder (Boys *et al.* 2003). The National Survey of Mental Health and Wellbeing conducted in Australia in 1998 found that cannabis use among 13- to 17-year-olds was associated with greater depression, conduct problems and health-risk behaviours such as smoking and drinking (Rey *et al.* 2002). Increasing levels of cannabis use are also associated with lower grade point averages at school (Resnick *et al.* 1997), less satisfaction with school (Brook *et al.* 1998), negative attitudes to school (Jones and Heaven 1998) and poor school performance (Novins and Mitchell 1998).

There are a number of possible explanations for these findings. First, the use of cannabis causes psychosocial problems through a variety of mechanisms. For example, cannabis may lead to poor educational performance by encouraging a range of anti-conventional behaviours such as

andel *et al.* 1986). Second, there is a reverse causal associa-
osocial problems prompting the use of cannabis. Accord-
edication' hypothesis, cannabis use develops in response
onditions such as psychotic illness as a means of coping
nptoms of the condition or the side effects of anti-psy-
(Dixon *et al.* 1990). Third, the relationship between
ychosocial functioning is non-causal and reflects the
risk factors. Analysing data from the Christchurch
ent Study cohort in New Zealand, Fergusson and
that individuals who reported using cannabis
more   ↗ to 16 were significantly more likely than
non-user   hosocial characteristics (e.g. socially
disadvantage   s with delinquent or substance-using pee   that are commonly associated with a greater m   blems. These three explanations have been exam   ospective, longitudinal
cohort studies that allow res   sh temporal priority (i.e.
does cannabis use precede or   ychosocial problems?) and
conduct analyses that control for the   cts of potentially confounding
variables. The findings of these studies will be considered in relation to
four main areas of psychosocial functioning: psychosis, depression,
educational attainment and antisocial or other problem behaviours.

Psychosis

Arseneault *et al.* (2004) reviewed the evidence for a causal association
between cannabis use and psychosis. The authors conducted a literature
search for studies that included samples drawn from population-based
registers or cohorts and used prospective measures of cannabis use and
adult psychosis. The search involved the Medline and Psyclit computerised databases, together with cross-referencing of the original studies
that were retrieved and contact with other researchers in this topic area.

Five studies, conducted in Sweden, New Zealand and the Netherlands, were included in the review. The Swedish study (Andreasson *et al.*
1987; Zammit *et al.* 2002) featured a cohort of just over 50,000 males
who were conscripted for compulsory military training in 1969–1970,
when almost all were aged 18 to 20 years. Conscripts completed

intelligence tests and self-reported questionnaires on family, social background and various aspects of behaviour in adolescence including substance use. All were interviewed by a psychologist, and those reporting any psychotic symptoms were subsequently assessed by a psychiatrist. Thirty-four individuals met the ICD-8 diagnostic criteria for psychosis (World Health Organization 1974) and were excluded from the remainder of the study. A total of 362 conscripts were later identified from the Swedish national hospital discharge register as having been hospitalized with a diagnosis of schizophrenia or paranoid psychosis during the period from 1970 to 1996.

The first of two studies from New Zealand (Arseneault *et al.* 2002) involved the birth cohort from the Dunedin Multidisciplinary Health and Development study. Cohort members were assessed for self-reported psychotic symptoms at the age of 11 years and substance use at ages 15 and 18, and took part in a standard diagnostic interview assessing schizophreniform disorder according to DSM-IV criteria (APA 1994) at age 26. Analyses were performed on 759 participants who provided complete data on all the relevant variables. The second study from New Zealand (Fergusson, Horwood and Swain-Campbell 2003c) analysed data from the Christchurch Health and Development Study birth cohort, with measures of DSM-IV cannabis dependence (APA 1994) and psychotic symptomatology (Symptom Checklist-90: Derogatis, Lipman and Covi 1973) recorded at the ages of 18 and 21 years, involving samples of 1025 and 1011 individuals, respectively.

The study by van Os *et al.* (2002) was based on data collected in the Netherlands Mental Health Survey and Incidence Study (NEMESIS), which assessed the prevalence, incidence, course and consequences of psychiatric disorders in the general population. A total of 7076 adults, aged 18 to 65 years, were recruited in 1996 and followed up over the next two years, with 4848 providing data at the final assessment. Psychotic symptoms and drug use were measured using the Composite International Diagnostic Interview (CIDI: Smeets and Dingemans 1993). All participants who reported psychotic symptoms at baseline or the first follow-up assessment were re-interviewed by an experienced clinician (e.g. psychiatrist or psychologist) over the telephone. In the event of a discrepancy between the diagnostic ratings of the clinician and the original lay interviewer, the former would be used to determine the participant's clinical status. The final assessment used the Brief Psychiatric Rating Scale (Overall and Gorham 1962) to measure the incidence of psychotic symptoms. Separate analyses were performed on data from 4045 participants who reported no symptoms of psychosis at the baseline measurement and a subsample of 59 individuals who had a DSM-III-R diagnosis of a psychotic disorder (APA 1987) at the first assessment.

Pooling the results from the five studies, Arseneault et al. (2004) found that individuals who had used cannabis were over two times more likely than non-users to report various psychosis-related outcomes. In the Swedish conscript study (Zammit et al. 2002), a total of 5391 individuals had reported cannabis use at the time of conscription and 73 (1.4% of the original sample) developed schizophrenia during the period from 1970 to 1996. Baseline users were 2.2 times more likely to have been diagnosed with schizophrenia than non-users of the drug. A similar association was found when the analyses were repeated on those participants who had used only cannabis and no other substances. Arseneault et al. (2002) noted that individuals from the Dunedin study sample who had used cannabis by the age of 18 had higher rates of schizophrenia symptoms than non-users at age 26. This association was stronger among participants who had used the drug before the age of 15. Users of cannabis prior to this age were also four times more likely to have a diagnosis of schizophreniform disorder in young adulthood. In the Christchurch Health and Development Study sample, Fergusson et al. (2003c) reported that individuals who met the diagnostic criteria for DSM-IV cannabis dependence disorder (APA 1994) at age 18 had rates of psychotic symptoms that were 3.7 times higher than those who were not dependent on the drug. At age 21, cannabis dependent participants were 2.3 times more likely than non-dependent individuals to report psychotic symptoms. In the NEMESIS study (van Os et al. 2002), 38 individuals reported psychotic symptoms at the final assessment, with ten classified as experiencing pathology-level psychosis, indicated by ratings of 4 to 7 on the Brief Psychiatric Rating Scale. Individuals who reported cannabis use at the baseline assessment were over three times more likely than non-users to report psychotic symptoms and over 28 times more likely to exhibit pathology-level psychosis. Baseline cannabis use was also more strongly associated with later psychotic symptoms than use of the drug reported at either of the follow-up assessments, which the authors interpreted as indicating that the association was not simply the result of the short-term effects of cannabis use.

Dose-response relationships were also observed in the Swedish and NEMESIS studies. Zammit *et al.* (2002) found that individuals reporting 'heavy' lifetime use (more than 50 times) at the time of conscription were over six times more likely than non-users to develop schizophrenia during the follow-up period, compared with a twofold increase in risk for those who had used the drug between five and ten times. In the NEMESIS study (van Os *et al.* 2002), frequency of cannabis use during the period of heaviest use was measured at each of the three assessments using a five-point scale, with 1 indicating 'nearly every day' and 5 'less than once a month'. Cumulative frequency of use was defined as the sum of the frequency ratings from all assessments, with scores of 1 to 5 indicating the highest level of use, 6 to 10 the middle level and 11 to 15 the lowest cumulative frequency. Participants in the high-level frequency category were over 11 times more likely than non-users to report psychotic symptoms, compared with a sevenfold increase in risk in the case of middle-level frequency.

Van Os *et al.* (2002) also conducted separate analyses on a group of 59 individuals who had received a DSM-III-R (APA 1987) diagnosis of any psychiatric disorder at the baseline assessment. Nine of these individuals reported using cannabis at the start of the study. The risk of reporting psychotic symptoms or pathology-level psychosis at follow-up was much higher among this group compared with the main sample of participants who had previously used cannabis but did not have a baseline psychiatric diagnosis. The increase in risk of reporting psychotic symptoms was 1.8% for the main sample and 46.7% for the baseline psychosis group. A similar pattern emerged for pathology-level psychosis, with an increase in risk of 2.2% for the main sample and 54.7% for those with baseline psychosis.

However, the most striking aspect of the findings in the review by Arseneault *et al.* (2004) was the impact of other variables on the relationship between cannabis use and psychosis-related outcomes. Although the associations in most cases remained significant after controlling for a variety of individual, family and social factors, their strength was often substantially reduced. For example, Zammit *et al.* (2002) conducted analyses that adjusted for the effects of psychiatric diagnoses at the time of conscription, IQ score, poor social integration, disturbed behaviour, cigarette smoking and place of upbringing. Heavy users of cannabis at the time of conscription were found to be three times more likely than non-users to develop schizophrenia, compared with a near sevenfold increase in risk in the unadjusted analyses. In the Dunedin study cohort (Arseneault *et al.* 2002), analyses that controlled for the level of psychotic symptoms measured at age 11 reduced the risk of schizophreniform disorder among cannabis users at age 15 by almost a third, so that the association was no longer statistically significant. A reduction in the strength of the association between cannabis use and psychotic symptoms was also noted by Fergusson *et al.* (2003c) after controlling for a range of factors including psychotic symptoms at the previous assessment, use of other substances, other mental health disorders and measures of social, family and individual functioning. A similar pattern was reported by van Os *et al.* (2002) following analyses adjusting for age, sex, ethnic group, marital status, educational level, urbanicity (population density), experience of discrimination and psychiatric diagnoses at baseline.

Arseneault *et al.* (2004) outlined a number of methodological limitations with the studies included in their review. A variety of measures were used to assess adult psychosis, so it is not possible to make any definitive statements about the role of cannabis use in specific mental health conditions such as schizophrenia. Cannabis use was measured using self-report and not confirmed by physiological tests such as urine or hair analyses, although this is likely to underestimate rather than inflate the strength of the observed relationships. Verdoux and Tournier (2004) have noted a number of additional limitations with these cohort studies. For example, neither the Swedish conscript (Andreasson *et al.* 1987; Zammit *et al.* 2002) nor the Dunedin study sample (Arseneault *et al.* 2002) collected data on substance use during the follow-up period, and the NEMESIS sample (van Os *et al.* 2002) featured only a small number of new cases of psychosis between the baseline and final assessments. Fergusson *et al.* (2003c) acknowledge that their study of the Christchurch cohort did not address the issue of the temporal sequencing of cannabis use and psychotic symptoms, as the data were collected and analysed separately at the two assessment points (ages 18 and 21).

However, the general pattern of findings is consistent with the view that cannabis use plays some causal role in the development of later psychosis. Cannabis users are more likely than non-users to report subsequent psychosis-related outcomes. The association appears stronger for higher frequency users, and the link remains significant, although reduced in strength, after controlling for the effects of previous psychotic symptoms and a range of other individual, family and social factors.

Smit, Boiler and Cuijpers (2004) assessed the evidence from four of the studies featured in the Arseneault et al. (2004) review and an additional historical cohort study from Israel (Weiser et al. 2002) in terms of five hypotheses that may be used to explain the relationship between cannabis and schizophrenia. These were the 'self-medication' hypothesis (schizophrenia causes cannabis use), other drugs (e.g. the effects of amphetamines or opiates), confounding (the effects of risk factors that are common to both cannabis use and schizophrenia), interaction (stronger associations among individuals with a predisposition for psychosis) and the aetiological hypothesis (cannabis plays a causal role in later psychosis). The authors concluded from the evidence that, while the self-medication and other drugs hypotheses may be discounted, the confounding hypothesis remains a possible explanation, since a large part of the association between cannabis use and schizophrenia is accounted for by other variables. In their review of the effects of drug use on young people under the age of 25 years, Macleod et al. (2004) note that the observed associations could still be accounted for by non-causal explanations, involving the effects of confounding variables not included in the analyses of these cohort studies. Rey, Martin and Krabman (2004) have commented that if cannabis does indeed double the risk of later psychosis, then the increase in the use of the drug that has occurred over the last fifty years should have been accompanied by a substantial rise in the number of people diagnosed with psychotic disorders. Degenhardt, Hall and Lynskey (2003a) analysed data from eight birth cohorts in Australia from 1940 to 1979 but did not find any evidence of an increase in the incidence of schizophrenia in line with the findings of the Arseneault et al. (2004) review.

Two recently published papers, however, have provided further evidence in support of a causal association between cannabis use and psychotic symptoms. Fergusson, Horwood and Ridder (2005) reported findings from the Christchurch Health and Development Study, involving data on the frequency of cannabis use and psychotic symptoms measured at the ages of 18, 21 and 25. Cohort members were questioned on their experiences of psychotic symptoms during the month prior to each assessment using the Symptom Checklist 90 (SCL-90) (Derogatis *et al.* 1973). They were also asked about their use of cannabis since the last assessment and frequency of use over the previous 12 months. Associations between cannabis use and psychotic symptoms were adjusted for the effects of a range of factors (e.g. family socio-economic circumstances, family functioning, child abuse and individual characteristics such as child neuroticism). Data analyses involved the 1055 participants for whom measures of cannabis use and psychotic symptoms were available from at least one of the three assessments between ages 18 and 25. At all ages, higher levels of cannabis use were associated with increasing rates of psychotic symptoms. After controlling for the effects of other variables, individuals reporting daily use of the drug had rates of psychotic symptoms that were between 1.6 and 1.8 times higher than those found among non-users. The results of analyses involving structural equation modelling suggested that these associations reflected the effects of cannabis use on symptom levels rather than the effects of symptom levels on cannabis use.

Henquet *et al.* (2005) examined the association between cannabis use and psychotic symptoms among individuals identified as having an above average predisposition for psychosis. Data were collected from a sample of 2437 14- to 24-year-olds participating in the Early Developmental Stages of Psychopathology study in Munich, Germany. Substance use, predisposition for psychosis and psychotic symptoms were assessed using the Munich version of the Composite International Diagnostic Interview (M-CIDI) (Wittchen *et al.* 1998a) and the Symptom Checklist (SCL-90-R) (Derogatis 1983) at the start of the study and again at follow-up four years later. For the purposes of the data analyses, 'exposure' to cannabis during adolescence was defined as reporting lifetime use of the drug five or more times at the baseline assessment, while cannabis use at follow-up was analysed as five times or more since baseline. Participants with total scores above the 90th centile of the paranoid ideation and psychoticism subscales of the SCL-90-R measure were classified as having a predisposition for psychosis.

At the follow-up assessment, 17.4% of participants reported at least one psychotic symptom since baseline. Earlier cannabis use was associated with an increased risk of psychotic symptoms at follow-up, with users of the drug being 1.79 times more likely than non-users to report psychotic symptoms. The risk was slightly reduced after controlling for the effects of age, sex, socio-economic status, urbanicity (i.e. population density), childhood trauma, predisposition for psychosis at baseline, and use of other drugs, tobacco and alcohol. There was also evidence of a dose-response relationship. Participants reporting cannabis use of three to four times a week at baseline were 2.44 times more likely than non-users to experience later psychotic symptoms, compared with those using the drug three to four times a month who were 1.5 times more likely. The association between baseline cannabis use and psychotic symptoms at follow-up was much stronger in those participants with a predisposition for psychosis at baseline than in those without. Just over half (51%) of cannabis users with the predisposition reported later psychotic symptoms, compared with 26% who had not used the drug. For those with no predisposition for psychosis, 21% of cannabis users reported psychotic symptoms at follow-up, compared with 15% who did not use the drug. The risk difference in the predisposition group was significantly greater than the risk difference found in the no predisposition group. There was no evidence in support of the 'self-medication' hypothesis, as a predisposition for psychosis recorded at baseline did not significantly predict cannabis use at follow-up.

There is some evidence that cannabis use can exacerbate the existing symptoms of schizophrenia. In their review of the clinical and epidemiological evidence on the association between cannabis and psychosis, Hall and Degenhardt (2000) cite a number of controlled studies that show poorer outcomes in terms of higher levels of psychotic symptoms and rates of hospitalisation among patients with schizophrenia who continued to use the drug (Cleghorn *et al.* 1991; Jablensky, Sartorius, Emberg *et al.* 1992; Negrete *et al.* 1986). Linszen, Dingemans and Lenior (1994) conducted a study featuring a sample of 93 individuals, aged 15 to 26 years, who were diagnosed as having schizophrenia or a related disorder using DSM-III-R criteria (APA 1987) and participating in a 15-month treatment programme. Twenty-four of the patients had a history of cannabis abuse. Psychotic, negative and affective symptoms of recent-onset schizophrenia and related disorders were assessed over the period of a year using the Brief Psychiatric Rating Scale (Overall and Gorham 1962). During the course of the study, cannabis abusers were more likely to relapse sooner and had more frequent relapses than patients who had not used the drug.

Depression

Degenhardt, Hall and Lynskey (2003b) conducted a search of the Medline, Psycinfo and Embase bibliographic databases to examine the evidence for an association between cannabis use and depression, and different explanations for this association. They concluded that the findings from most longitudinal cohort studies did not support the 'self-medication' hypothesis – that is, an increased risk of later cannabis use among individuals who are depressed (Bardone *et al.* 1998; Brook, Cohen and Brook 1998; Hofstra, van der Ende and Verhultz 2002; Kandel and Chen 2000; Kandel and Davies 1986; Miller-Johnson *et al.* 1998; Patton *et al.* 2002; Weissman, Wolk, Wickramaratne *et al.* 1999). However, there was some evidence of an association between adolescent depression and later use of the drug. A study by Paton, Kessler and Kandel (1977) featured a random sample of over 8000 adolescents from 18 public secondary schools in New York State, US, who were assessed in terms of their depressive mood and illicit drug use at two timepoints, five to six months apart. Depressive mood was related to the onset of marijuana use among those who were non-users at baseline, but was also associated with a greater likelihood of ceasing use among baseline users. McGee, Williams, Poulton *et al.* (2000) examined the relationship between cannabis use and a range of mental health disorders, including depression, by analysing data from the Dunedin Multidisciplinary Health and Development Study (DMHDS) in New Zealand. Cannabis use at the age of 15 was assessed in terms of the frequency of use during the previous year (never, once or twice, or three or more times), and at ages 18 and 21 in terms of frequency and also dependence according to DSM-III-R criteria (APA 1994). Mental health disorders at all ages were assessed using the Diagnostic Interview Schedule for Children (DISC-C: Costello, Edelbrock, Kalas *et al.* 1982) and the parent-completed Revised Behavior Problem Checklist (RBPC: Quay and Peterson 1987). The analyses indicated that mental disorder recorded at age 15 was associated with a small but significant increase in risk of cannabis use by the age of 18.

The review by Degenhardt *et al.* (2003b) cited a number of studies that found significant associations between adolescent cannabis use and later depression, other mental health disorders and suicide attempts, although part of this relationship was explained by the effects of confounding variables (Fergusson and Horwood 1997; Fergusson, Horwood and Swain-Campbell 2002; McGee *et al.* 2000; Patton *et al.* 2002). In their analysis of data from the DMHDS cohort, McGee *et al.* (2000) noted that, while cannabis use by age 15 was not associated with an increased risk of mental disorder at age 18, use of the drug among 18-year-olds did predict a greater likelihood of mental disorder at the age of 21, although for male participants only.

Findings from another New Zealand cohort, the Christchurch Health and Development Study, were reported by Fergusson and Horwood (1997), who examined the relationship between cannabis use prior to the age of 16 and various indicators of psychosocial adjustment, including mental health problems, at age 18. Symptoms of depression and anxiety that occurred during the period from ages 16 to 18 were assessed using a questionnaire based on the Composite International Diagnostic Interview (CIDI: World Health Organization 1993). Participants were also asked about suicidal behaviours during this period. Analyses were performed on a sample of 935 respondents (73.9% of the original cohort sample) who provided complete data on the relevant variables. The use of cannabis on ten or more occasions prior to age 16 was associated with significantly increased risks of major depression and suicide attempts between the ages of 16 and 18. For example, 45.8% of participants who had used the drug ten or more times prior to age 16 met the criteria for major depressive disorder at age 18, compared with 18.4% of those who had never used the drug. Around a fifth of high frequency users (20.8%)

reported making a suicide attempt between ages 16 and 18, compared with 14.4% of never-users. However, the increased risks for these mental health outcomes among cannabis users were no longer statistically significant after controlling for the effects of individual, family, peer and socio-demographic variables.

Fergusson *et al.* (2002) re-examined the association between cannabis use and mental health outcomes in the Christchurch cohort by including data collected between the ages of 14 and 21. Analyses were performed on data from 1063 sample members, representing 84% of the original cohort. There were significant relationships between the frequency of cannabis use and rates of depression, suicidal ideation and suicidal attempts. However, adjustment for the effects of a range of confounding factors (e.g. socio-demographic and individual characteristics, adverse life events, peer affiliations, school and home leaving age and alcohol dependence) reduced the strength of the relationships. Following this adjustment, participants who reported using cannabis at least once a week in any given year between the ages of 14 and 21 were nearly two times more likely than non-users to be diagnosed with depression. Weekly cannabis use was also associated with an increased risk of suicidal ideation and attempts, although there was an interaction effect between cannabis use and age, with a stronger association at ages 14 to 15. Weekly users of cannabis in this age group were around seven times more likely than non-users to report suicidal thoughts and had rates of suicide attempts that were approximately 13 times higher than those of non-users. By the ages of 20 to 21, however, there was no longer a significant association between weekly cannabis use and suicidal behaviours.

Patton *et al.* (2002) investigated the relationship between adolescent cannabis use and rates of depression and anxiety at the ages of 20 to 21 in the Victorian Adolescent Health Cohort Study in Australia. Cannabis use was measured at six assessment points during years 9 to 12 of secondary school. Mental health outcomes were measured using the Revised Clinical Interview Schedule (CIS-R: Lewis and Pelosi 1992), with a score of 12 or greater indicating a mixed state of depression and anxiety where clinical intervention is considered appropriate. A total of 1601 individuals, representing 79% of the original sample, provided data at the young adulthood assessment, with 71 males and 188 females reporting depression and anxiety. Females who had used cannabis more than once a week during adolescence were 2.6 times more likely than non-using females to report depression and anxiety in young adulthood. This association persisted, although somewhat reduced in strength, after controlling for the effects of a number of confounding variables, including levels of depression and anxiety in adolescence, alcohol use, antisocial behaviour, parental separation and parental education.

Educational attainment

Lynskey and Hall (2000) summarised the research on relationships between cannabis use and various indicators of educational attainment, such as truancy, not completing compulsory schooling, and leaving school without any formal qualifications. The authors identified longitudinal studies of these variables through a search of the medical, psychological, educational and economic literatures, checking the reference lists of the retrieved articles, and citation searches of early key articles.

Fergusson, Lynskey and Horwood (1996) reported on the association between the use of cannabis prior to the age of 15 years and a variety of psychosocial outcomes, including truancy and school dropout, at ages 15 to 16 in the Christchurch Health and Development Study cohort in New Zealand. Participants with either self-reports or parental reports of cannabis use at ages 14 or 15 were classified as users of the drug. Frequent truancy from ages 15 to 16 was defined as being truant on 15 or more occasions during this period based on self-reports or parental reports. Any participant who had left school before the minimum leaving age of 16 was classified as a school dropout. A total of 927 cohort members provided complete data on the outcomes measured at age 16. Around one in ten participants had used cannabis by the age of 15 and this group had significantly higher rates of truancy and school dropout than non-users. Nearly a third (31.5%) of users reported frequent truancy compared with 4.7% of non-users, while 22.5% had left school before the age of 16 compared with only 3.5% of non-users. Associations between early cannabis use and these outcomes were adjusted for the effects of a range of potential confounding variables, which included family social background (e.g. family social position, functioning, history of substance abuse), childhood behaviour problems and cognitive ability recorded at age 8, commitment to education, peer affiliations and psychosocial adjustment. After controlling for these factors, the relationship between cannabis use before the age of 15 and school dropout was still significant, although the risk had decreased, with users being just over three times more likely than non-users to have left school before the age of 16. However, the relationship between early use and truancy was no longer significant.

A follow-up analysis of the Christchurch cohort was reported by Fergusson and Horwood (1997), examining the relationship between cannabis use at ages 15 to 16 and leaving school without any formal qualifications during the period from ages 16 to 18. Just under a fifth (18.7%) of the 935 respondents who provided complete data on the outcome measures had left school without any qualifications by age 18. Cannabis use was associated with an increased risk of leaving school without qualifications. Over half (54.2%) of the 48 participants who had used cannabis more than ten times at ages 15 and 16 had no qualifications on leaving school compared with 30.3% of those who had used the drug one to nine times and 14.4% of non-users. The relationship between cannabis use and educational attainment remained significant after adjustment for a range of family, social, individual and peer-related factors, although the strength of the association was substantially reduced.

The effect of early adolescent drug use on the likelihood of completing schooling was also examined by Ellickson et al. (1998). This study featured a sample of over 4000 pupils from 30 schools in the states of California and Oregon, US, who were participating in the RAND Adolescent Panel Study. Students were first surveyed in the seventh grade and then again five years later. Frequency of alcohol, cigarette and marijuana use was assessed, together with a range of potentially confounding factors, including demographic characteristics, family structure, academic orientation, early deviance and school environment. Although the initial analyses showed an increased risk of dropping out of high school among marijuana users, this association was no longer significant after controlling for other variables. However, separate analyses for the four ethnic groups comprising the sample found that earlier marijuana use was associated with an increased likelihood of dropping out of high school for Latino pupils, even after controlling for the effects of other factors.

Two additional studies of cannabis use and educational attainment were cited by Rey *et al.* (2004) in their review of the cannabis literature among children and adolescents. The study by Fergusson, Horwood and Beautrais (2003a) was a further follow-up assessment of the Christchurch cohort at the age of 25. At each assessment from ages 15 to 25, cohort members were questioned about their use of cannabis, including frequency of use and any problems related to their use, during the time since the previous assessment. At ages 18, 21 and 25, participants were asked about their educational achievements, including whether they had left school without any formal qualifications by the age of 18, enrolled in university by the age of 21, and attained a university degree by the age of 25. The results indicated that participants who had used marijuana on at least 100 occasions by the age of 16 were nearly six times more likely to leave school without qualifications than those who had never used the drug. Compared with high frequency users, those who had never used cannabis by age 18 were around three times more likely to enter university than high frequency users, and 'never-users' at age 21 were 4.5 times more likely to attain a degree. Analyses that adjusted for confounding social, family and childhood factors reduced the association between earlier cannabis use and leaving school without any formal qualifications, but the relationship remained statistically significant. Those who had used cannabis on more than 100 occasions by the age of 16 were 3.7 times more likely than never-users to leave school without formal qualifications. However, the association between earlier cannabis use and university enrolment was no longer significant and, in the case of degree attainment, was only marginally significant.

Lynskey *et al.* (2003) examined the relationship between weekly cannabis use during adolescence and early school leaving in the Victorian Adolescent Health Cohort Study in Australia. Data on self-reported cannabis use were collected at six time points during a three-year period between ages 15 and 18 and then again at age 21. The results showed that young people who used cannabis weekly were more likely than non-users to leave school early (i.e. before year 12). The association was strongest among younger students. In year 10, weekly cannabis users were almost six times more likely than non-users to leave school early, in year 11 they were around three times more likely, and by year 12 they were nearly two times more likely. After controlling for the effects of a range of covariates including demographic characteristics, other substance use (cigarette smoking and alcohol consumption), antisocial behaviour and psychiatric morbidity, weekly cannabis use in year 10 was associated with a 5.6-fold increase in the risk of early school leaving. By year 12, however, there was no longer an association between weekly use and early school leaving.

The findings of the longitudinal studies reviewed by Lynskey and Hall (2000) suggest that the use of cannabis may play some causal role in poor educational performance, given that the association between the two variables persists even after controlling for a range of confounding variables. However, the possibility remains that the association is non-causal and may reflect the impact of other variables not accounted for in these studies. Lynskey and Hall (2000) outline a number of explanations for a causal relationship between cannabis use and early school leaving. The 'amotivational syndrome' describes a collection of symptoms including apathy, lethargy, lack of motivation, and impairments in memory, concentration and judgement, which is associated with the long-term heavy use of cannabis (Brill and Nahas 1984; McGlothin and West 1968; Smith 1968). However, Hall, Solowij and Lemon (1994) have stated that much of the evidence for this syndrome is in the form of case histories and observational reports. It is possible that cannabis use may increase the risk of early school leaving by an impairment of cognitive functioning, although Solowij (1999) has noted that use of the drug does not cause gross cognitive deficits. A more likely explanation proposed by Fergusson and Horwood (1997) is that cannabis use occurs within a peer group that encourages adolescents to adopt other non-conventional behaviours and assume more adult roles, which then increases the likelihood of early school leaving. This hypothesis is consistent with the results of a number of studies that have found an association between adolescent cannabis use and behaviours such as early sexual activity (Rosenbaum and Kandel 1990), unplanned parenthood (Krohn, Lizotte, Perez 1997; Mensch and Kandel 1988), unemployment (Fergusson and Horwood 1997) and leaving the family home early (Fergusson and Horwood 1997; Krohn et al. 1997).

Antisocial and other problem behaviours

Derzon and Lipsey (1999) conducted a meta-analysis of the findings from prospective, longitudinal studies that examined the relationship between marijuana use and delinquent or other problem behaviours. Studies were identified from a search of computerised databases, snowball sampling of retrieved papers and review bibliographies, and the scanning of conference proceedings. A total of 63 reports describing 30 studies were identified, from which 511 effect sizes of the relationship between marijuana use and delinquent behaviour were coded. Almost 90% of the effect sizes were from studies conducted in the US and a similar percentage involved self-report data. A total of 374 effect sizes referred to cross-sectional relationships, 68 involved the measurement of marijuana use prior to delinquent and problem behaviour, and 60 involved the measurement of delinquent and problem behaviour prior to marijuana use. Effect sizes were examined in five categories of delinquent behaviour: aggressive behaviour, problem behaviour, mixed offences, property offences and person offences.

The general pattern of results showed a positive correlation between marijuana and delinquent behaviours, with higher use associated with more delinquent behaviours, although the overall strength of the relationship between the variables was not large. The strongest relationships were found when marijuana use and delinquent behaviours were measured concurrently. In three of the five categories ('problem behaviour', 'mixed offences', 'person offences'), the cross-sectional effect sizes were larger than those for longitudinal relationships. However, for every category with data, stronger associations were found when problem behaviours were measured before marijuana use. Mean effect sizes were often two or more times larger than when marijuana use predicted problem behaviours. Derzon and Lipsey (1999) concluded that the nature of the relationship between marijuana use and delinquent behaviours is likely to be one of co-morbidity rather than cause and effect.

Macleod *et al.* (2004) summarised the findings on antisocial behaviours from general population longitudinal studies in their wider review of associations between illicit drug use and psychosocial harm. Studies were identified through a search of electronic bibliographic databases (e.g. Medline, Embase, Cinahl, Psyclit, Web of Science), specialist databases (e.g. Drugscope) and contacts with key individuals in the speciality of addictions. The review concluded that there was an inconsistent association between cannabis use and antisocial or otherwise problematic behaviour.

Among the studies cited in the Macleod *et al.* (2004) review were a series of analyses from the Christchurch Health and Development Study in New Zealand. Fergusson *et al.* (1996) reported on the association between early-onset cannabis use and various adjustment problems, including juvenile offending, during the period from ages 15 to 16. At age 16, cohort members and their parents were questioned about the young person's offending behaviours in the previous year using the Self-Report Delinquency Scale (Moffitt and Silva 1988). Individuals were classified as recurrent offenders if they, or their parents, reported that the young person had committed five or more offences involving property offences or violence in the last year. Information on official police contacts during the ages 15 to 16 period was also obtained, following signed parental consent for access to police records. The analyses were based on 927 cohort members, representing 83.4% of the original Christchurch cohort, who provided complete data on the outcomes measured at age 16. Those who had used cannabis by the age of 15 had significantly higher rates of repeat offending (25.8%) than non-users (5.7%) and were also more likely to have had contacts with the police (20.3%) than non-users (5.0%). However, after controlling for possible confounding variables (e.g. family functioning, association with delinquent or substance-using peers, other substance use) and correction for multiple significance tests, the association between early cannabis use and both indicators of delinquency was no longer significant.

Fergusson and Horwood (1997) performed a follow-up analysis of the Christchurch cohort at age 18. Participants were questioned about their offending behaviours and contact with the criminal justice system over the period from ages 17 to 18 years using the Self Report Delinquency Inventory (Elliott and Huizinga 1989) and survey items concerning the number of police contacts and the consequences of these contacts. Analyses were performed on data from 935 respondents. The results showed that those participants who reported frequent use of cannabis (ten or more occasions) by age 16 had a greater risk than non-users of juvenile offending during the period from ages 16 to 18. For example, the rate of court convictions among frequent users was 31.3% compared with 2.4% of non-users, and the level of repeat violent offending (three or more times) was 33.3% for frequent users compared with 6.2% of non-users. This association remained statistically significant, although with reduced strength, after controlling for the effects of confounding social, family and childhood variables. An additional analysis of the same cohort conducted at the age of 21 (Fergusson *et al.* 2002) found highly significant associations between the frequency of cannabis use and rates of violent or property offending over the period from 14 to 21 years. However, these relationships were again reduced in strength following adjustment for other factors. At the ages of 14 to 15 years, weekly cannabis users had rates of property or violent crime that were 3.7 times those of non-users. The strength of the association between cannabis use and offending was lower for older cohort members.

Summary

Cross-sectional surveys have found that the use of cannabis is associated with a range of psychosocial outcomes, including psychosis, depression, poor educational performance and antisocial behaviour. There are a number of possible explanations for these relationships. Cannabis may cause the development of psychosocial problems, the use of the drug may develop in response to these problems (reverse causation), or the association may be non-causal and result from the impact of risk factors that are common to both cannabis use and psychosocial functioning. These explanations have been examined in a number of longitudinal studies featuring prospective measures of cannabis and psychosocial variables, together with statistical analyses that control for the effects of possible confounding factors.

The evidence is consistent with the view that cannabis plays some causal role in the development of psychosis. Cannabis users are more likely than non-users to report a variety of psychosis-related outcomes, and the association is stronger for higher frequency users and for those with a predisposition for psychosis in early adolescence. The link remains statistically significant, although reduced in strength, after controlling for the effects of previous psychotic symptoms and a range of other individual, family and social factors. There remains the possibility that the association between cannabis use and psychosis is non-causal and attributable to the effects of additional variables that have not been accounted for in the studies. There is some evidence that cannabis use can exacerbate the existing symptoms of schizophrenia among adolescents.

Part of the relationship between cannabis use and other areas of psychosocial functioning, including depression, educational attainment and antisocial behaviours, can also be attributed to the effects of other variables. Even after controlling for these factors, however, a number of longitudinal studies have found that cannabis users are at a greater risk than non-users of being diagnosed with a depressive disorder, reporting suicidal thoughts and attempting suicide. They are also more likely to truant from school, drop out of school, leave school without any formal qualifications, and are at an increased risk of juvenile offending.

6 Cannabis and the Use of Other Illicit Drugs

The 'gateway' effect

A further source of public concern over the use of cannabis by young people is the possibility that it may act as a 'gateway' to experimentation with and the regular use of other illicit drugs such as cocaine or opiates that are potentially more harmful (Kandel, Yamaguchi and Chen 1992). A number of studies have noted an association between the use of cannabis and other substances. In the National Survey of Mental Health and Wellbeing conducted in Australia in 1998, Rey *et al.* (2002) found that of the 319 adolescents who reported using cannabis at least once during their lives, 39% had tried other illicit drugs compared with 12% of those who had never used cannabis. Perkonigg *et al.* (1999) reported findings from the sample of 14- to 17-year-olds participating in the Early Developmental Stages of Psychopathology Study in Germany. Among the 212 individuals who reported using cannabis at least once at the start of the study, 17.5% also reported the use of other drugs. The most commonly reported substances were amphetamines (9.4%), followed by hallucinogens (6.1%) and cocaine (5.2%). At the time of the follow-up assessment, an average of 19.7 months later, 28.9% of those who had continued to use cannabis also reported other drug use, with amphetamines again being the most commonly use substance (17.4%). Rates of other drug use were even higher among those with a DSM-IV (APA 1994) diagnosis of cannabis abuse (61.3%) or dependence (66.7%). The proportion of respondents who reported using three or more different types of drug during the previous 12 months was 9.4% among continuous cannabis users, 19.4% for those diagnosed as cannabis abusers and 50% for cannabis dependent individuals.

The use of cannabis may act as a 'gateway' to other substances in a number of ways (MacCoun 1998). Some users who experience positive effects with cannabis may try other drugs to see if they have similar effects. Interaction with drug-using peers and dealers may bring them into contact with other drugs, and this environment may encourage the use of these other substances. However, the links between cannabis and other illicit drug use may be non-causal. It may reflect the influence of common risk factors (e.g. delinquency) or a general propensity to use drugs. Those with such a propensity use cannabis before other substances because it is more readily available.

In their systematic review of the literature on longitudinal studies of drug use and psychosocial harm, Macleod *et al.* (2004) concluded that the use of cannabis was consistently associated with the use of other drugs. Among the included studies were a number of analyses of data from the Christchurch Health and Development Study in New Zealand. Fergusson and Horwood (1997) reported on the findings of the assessments conducted at ages 16 and 18. At 16, cohort members were asked about their use of cannabis during the previous year and at the following assessment gave details of their use of other substances during the previous two years. A range of potentially confounding variables were also measured, including socio-economic background, family functioning, parental adjustment, individual characteristics (e.g. cognitive ability, conduct problems, self-esteem, novelty seeking), early adolescent adjustment, peer affiliations, risk-taking and lifestyle. A total of 935 individuals provided data on the relevant variables at both assessments. Almost one in ten of the cohort reported using other drugs during this period, including solvents (2.5%) and hallucinogenics (3.5%). Higher levels of cannabis use before the age of 16 were associated with an increased risk of other drug use at age 18. The rate of other substance use among those who used cannabis ten or more times was 62.5%, compared with 20.5% for those using cannabis one to nine times, and 4.2% for non-users. The association between earlier cannabis use and subsequent other drug use remained statistically significant, although reduced in strength after controlling for other factors.

A follow-up analysis was conducted at age 21 (Fergusson and Horwood 2000b). A total of 990 cohort members provided complete data on the relevant variables covering the period from ages 15 to 21. By the age of 21, 69% had used cannabis at least once during their lives and 26.3% reported the use of other illicit drugs. Of the 246 respondents who had used other drugs, all but three had used cannabis first. However, 63% of cannabis users had never tried other drugs. Analyses of the association between cannabis and other illicit drug use was performed using a proportional hazards model. The hazard or risk of illicit drug use was modelled as a function of the level of cannabis use in any given year between the ages of 15 and 21. The analyses showed that there was a significant association between the reporting of cannabis use in any given year and the onset of illicit drug use, with a stronger association for higher levels of cannabis use. Participants who reported using cannabis on one or two occasions had hazards of other illicit drug use that were 3.5 times higher than those who did not use cannabis, while those using cannabis 50 or more times had hazards of other drug use that were 143 times higher. Only 0.3% of those individuals who had not used cannabis by the age of 21 reported using other illicit drugs, compared with 78% of those reporting cannabis use on at least 50 occasions in any given year. After adjustment for a range of potentially confounding factors, cannabis use remained strongly related to the onset of other forms of illicit drug use, with those using cannabis on more than 50 occasions a year having hazards of other illicit drug use that were 59.2 times higher than non-users.

Fergusson and Horwood (2000b) concluded that the findings of the analyses were consistent with the notion of cannabis as a gateway to other forms of illicit drug use. However, they acknowledged the possibility of a non-causal explanation of the results due to factors that were either not present or inadequately controlled for in the analyses. Furthermore, Morral, McCaffrey and Paddock (2002) have constructed a statistical model of data from the US National Household Survey of Drug Abuse to show how the associations between marijuana and other illicit drug use can be explained in terms of a general drug use propensity rather than a gateway effect.

A further analysis of data at age 21 (Fergusson *et al.* 2002) showed a clear reduction in the association between cannabis and other drug use with age. The association was particularly strong at ages 14 to 15, with weekly users over 230 times more likely than non-users to report the use of other drugs after controlling for other factors. By ages 20 to 21, however, weekly cannabis users were 12 times more likely than non-users to report other drug use.

Miller and Volk (1996) have conducted one of the few studies examining links between cannabis and a specific illicit drug, namely cocaine. The study featured data collected from the National Youth Survey (NYS) over six assessment periods. The NYS was a national probability sample of households in the US beginning in 1976 (Elliott, Huizinga and Ageton 1985). All youths aged 11 to 17 years on December 31, 1976, were eligible for inclusion in the study. A total of 1725 individuals participated in the initial survey, with interviews conducted at annual intervals over the next four years, and an additional two-year follow-up in 1983. In addition to recording levels of substance use (cigarettes, alcohol, marijuana and cocaine), the survey also included a number of psychosocial measures based on an integrated theoretical model of substance use devised by Elliott, Huizinga and Menard (1989). These included strain (the discrepancy between the individual's aspirations and achievements), conventional bonding (their attachment to family, school and societal norms) and deviant peer bonding (the extent of their involvement with friends who engage in deviant behaviours).

Discrete-time survival analysis was employed to determine whether marijuana use was a risk factor for later cocaine use. The results of the analyses were presented for three groups according to their ages at the time of the initial interview (11 to 13, 14 to 15, and 16 to 17). Concurrent and prior weekly marijuana use were found to be significant predictors of subsequent cocaine use among all three age groups, with the exception of those aged 16 to 17 at the start of the study, with only prior weekly use being a significant predictor. In all cases, the association with cocaine use was stronger for prior weekly marijuana use than concurrent weekly use. The association between weekly marijuana use and cocaine use persisted after adjusting for the effects of the other psychosocial variables, although the reporting of deviant attitudes, an element of the deviant peer bonding measure, significantly reduced the strength of this association.

Summary

An additional source of public concern over the use of cannabis among adolescents is the possibility that it may lead to the use of other illicit drugs. Evidence in support of this 'gateway' effect comes from the Christchurch Health and Development Study in New Zealand. In the most recent analyses conducted when the cohort was aged 21, the reporting of cannabis use in any given year between the ages of 14 and 21 was associated with an increased risk of other illicit drug use, with a stronger association for higher levels of cannabis use but weaker associations with increasing age. The relationship remained significant after adjustment for a range of potential confounding factors. However, there remains the possibility of a non-causal explanation of the results due to factors that were either not present or inadequately controlled for in the analyses. An analysis of data from the NYS in the US has also found an increased risk of cocaine use among adolescents who reported prior weekly use of cannabis.

7 Prevention and Treatment

Prevention

Drug prevention programmes are of two major types: universal and targeted (Christian *et al.* 2001). Universal programmes involve all young people, while targeted interventions are for those who are judged to be at increased risk of drug misuse, have already tried drugs or show risk-related problem behaviours. Although the majority of preventive interventions are school-based, some also involve the wider community or are delivered via the mass media (e.g. television campaigns).

The literature on drug prevention programmes is immense, with one systematic review alone evaluating the effects of 125 interventions (White and Pitts 1998). The focus of this chapter will be studies that deal specifically with cannabis-related outcomes.

School-based interventions

Tobler *et al.* (1999) examined the effectiveness of school-based drug prevention in relation to marijuana use by conducting a meta-analysis of the findings from 37 programmes. A comprehensive literature search for programmes was conducted, involving computer databases, purchased dissertations, existing literature reviews and bibliographies, letters to national drug abuse programme directors and research grant recipients, and telephone inquiries. The inclusion criteria were universal, school-based drug prevention programmes that were open to all ethnic groups, implemented between the sixth and twelfth grades, and conducted in the US and Canada between 1978 and 1991. Both randomised and non-randomised studies were included, although the latter only if they had pre-test and post-test results for both the experimental and comparison groups. Treatment programmes targeting addicted youth were excluded. The literature search identified 595 studies of adolescent prevention programmes. A total of 30 studies, detailing 37 programmes featuring marijuana use outcomes, met these inclusion criteria.

For the purposes of the meta-analysis, the included programmes were divided into two groups, interactive (22 programmes) and non-interactive (15 programmes), based on their content and the form of delivery. Interactive programmes emphasised interpersonal competence and the acquisition of drug refusal skills, with the programme leader in the role of a facilitator rather than teacher. Non-interactive programmes focused on increasing knowledge of drug-related issues (e.g. effects, media and social influences, peer use) and improving intrapersonal functioning (e.g. self-esteem, personal insight, self-awareness) within a more passive learning approach.

Programme type and sample size were found to be significant predictors of programme effectiveness. Non-interactive programmes showed minimal reductions in marijuana use. Interactive programmes, however, showed greater reductions and also had a significant impact on attitudes. Larger implementations of both programme types (more than 400 students) were less effective than smaller ones, although the larger interactive programmes were significantly more effective than the larger non-interactive ones.

A recent example of an interactive intervention is described by Duncan *et al.* (2000). The 'Refuse To Use' programme was presented in a CD-ROM format and consisted of a series of video vignettes, each depicting a common situation in which an offer of marijuana might be made to adolescents, together with a number of choices for how this offer might be refused. An evaluation of the programme involved a total of 74 public school students from six classes in three high schools in the state of Oregon, US. Students were from the ninth to twelfth grades with a mean age of 15.2 years. One class from each school was randomly chosen as a control classroom, with a second class serving as the experimental group. Immediately prior to the use of the programme, students completed a brief 11-item survey, which asked about their perceived efficacy of drug refusal skills (e.g. 'if someone you didn't know offered you marijuana at a party, how confident are you that you could refuse?'), intentions to refuse drugs (e.g. 'if offered marijuana in the next six months, how likely is it that you would refuse the offer?') and social norms for using or refusing drugs (e.g. 'if I don't smoke marijuana I will feel left out of a group'). The teacher then presented the programme to the class on a large monitor. The class interacted with the programme collectively, making the decisions requested by the programme as a group. On the following day, a brief post-test survey was administered. Data from 65 participants (27 in the experimental condition and 38 in the control) were included in the data analyses.

Significant changes were observed at post-test on a number of the outcomes. Students in the intervention group reported significantly greater efficacy about their refusal skills and intentions to refuse marijuana than participants in the control condition. Those who received the intervention were also more likely to agree that if an individual refused a drug offer it would be unreasonable for the person offering the drug to continue pressuring them to use it. There was a significant treatment by gender interaction for the perceived importance of respecting another individual's decision to refuse a drug offer. Females in the intervention group placed greater importance on respecting that decision than did females in the control condition.

Many school-based programmes focus on changing attitudes and skills at the individual level but do not address the state of the wider school environment and the impact that this can have on students' behaviour and well-being. The study by Bond *et al.* (2004) provides details of the 'Gatehouse Project', which includes both institutional and individual-level components designed to promote the well-being of secondary school pupils in Melbourne, Australia. The individual component of the programme, a curriculum taught over the course of a ten-week school term, included cognitive and interpersonal skills relevant to students' emotional well-being but no specific drug education skills. The institutional components included a school-based adolescent health team, the use of student surveys to identify risk and protective factors related to well-being in the school environment, and strategies to address these factors.

Bond *et al.* (2004) examined the impact of the Gatehouse Project on the prevalence and incidence of cannabis use recorded over a two and a half year period. Twenty-six out of a total of 32 schools (12 from districts randomly allocated to receive the intervention and 14 from districts with control group status) agreed to participate in the evaluation. Baseline data were collected at the beginning of year 8, when the average age of the students was 13.4 years, with follow-up assessments conducted at the end of years 8, 9 and 10. Cannabis use was assessed in terms of self-reported frequency during the six months prior to each assessment. Additional measures included socio-demographic details, self-reported alcohol and tobacco use, and school engagement, an indicator of student disaffection with the school environment. Data were collected from 2678 students (74% of those eligible to participate) at the first assessment, and 2145 provided complete data for the final analyses two and a half years later.

After controlling for the effects of baseline cannabis use, gender, family structure and school engagement, the analyses showed only a modest effect of the intervention on the prevalence of cannabis use, with 18.6% of the intervention group reporting lifetime use of the drug, compared with 21.5% of the control group. Similar patterns were found when comparing the two groups in terms of incidence rates (i.e. new cases of cannabis use since baseline) and the prevalence of weekly cannabis use. The analyses revealed a significant interaction effect between intervention group and tobacco smoking at baseline for the number of new cases of weekly cannabis use. This finding suggested that the impact of the intervention on incident weekly use was greater for non-smokers at baseline than it was for students who already smoked.

Community-based components

Stevens, Freeman, Mott *et al.* (1996) studied the effects on marijuana use of a combined school and community-based drug prevention curriculum, in comparison with the school-based curriculum alone and a control community. Four rural school districts in rural New Hampshire, US, agreed to participate and were assigned, although not in a random manner, to one of the two interventions or control group status. The school-based intervention featured the 'Here's Looking at You, 2000' curriculum, which was used in conjunction with a parenting course and community task force for the combined intervention group (Stevens *et al.* 1993). The aim of this curriculum was to develop students' personal and social skills in a range of areas and by a variety of methods including demonstration, behavioural rehearsal, feedback and reinforcement. The parenting course was designed to help parents communicate more effectively with their children about risky or unacceptable behaviour, including drug use. The function of the community task force was to work with the police, schools and other community groups to promote awareness of and changes in attitudes and behaviour relating to drug use.

A total of 1200 school children, aged 9 to 14, participated in the study and were followed up annually over three years. Questionnaires were completed at each follow-up, detailing drug use, attitudes and beliefs about drugs and psychosocial risk factors for drugs. Complete data were obtained from 80.9% of the original sample. The analyses showed that there were no differences between the three groups in terms of the likelihood of students starting to use marijuana. However, after adjusting for the effects of demographic (e.g. gender, age, school grade) and psychosocial (e.g. school satisfaction, academic achievement, depression) variables, students in the combined school and community intervention group were less likely than those in the control group to report regular marijuana smoking during the course of the study.

Mass media interventions

Palmgreen *et al.* (2001) evaluated the effectiveness of the SENTAR (sensation seeking targeting) media campaigns in reducing marijuana use among high-sensation seeking adolescents. Sensation seeking is a personality trait that is characterised by a need for novel, complex, ambiguous and emotionally intense stimuli, and is associated with an increased risk of drug use (Zuckerman 1994).

The study used a controlled interrupted time-series design. Anti-marijuana public service announcements developed specifically for high-sensation seekers were televised from January to April 1997 in Fayette County, Kentucky, with Knox County, Tennessee, serving as the control comparison. This was followed by a booster campaign from January to April 1998 involving both counties. Each announcement featured one or more of the possible consequences of using marijuana, including lung damage and psychological and physical dependence (Stephenson *et al.* 1999). Interviews with a randomly selected sample of 100 students, initially in the seventh to tenth grades, were conducted in each county eight months before the start of the first campaign and again every month for the next 32 months until after the 1998 campaign. The interviews assessed a range of topics including exposure to the announcements, marijuana-related beliefs and attitudes and use of the drug in the previous 30 days. Sensation seeking was measured with the Brief Sensation Seeking Scale. Respondents scoring higher or lower than the full-sample medians were classified as high- and low-sensation seekers, respectively.

The analyses showed that low-sensation seekers in both counties reported low levels of marijuana use throughout the 32-month period of data collection. In the case of high-sensation seekers, marijuana use increased steadily prior to the start of the SENTAR campaigns. A significant decline in use was observed following the introduction of the first campaign in Fayette County, which continued until around six months after the campaign. This was followed by a significant rise in 30-day use, which persisted for around five months and then began to fall again shortly before the end of the second campaign. Marijuana use in Knox County showed a significant downward trend after the start of the 1998 campaign, which continued for the remainder of the data collection period.

Treatment for cannabis users

The demand for the treatment of cannabis-related problems has increased in recent years. A review of this area by Copeland (2004) notes that the number of individuals in Australia seeking treatment for their cannabis use doubled between 2000/01 and 2001/02, with people under the age of 20 accounting for nearly half of these cases (AIHW 2003). In 2000, the US Treatment Episode Data Set reported that cannabis accounted for 61% of all adolescent admissions to publicly funded substance abuse treatment facilities (SAMHSA 2003). Despite this growing demand, the evidence base for the treatment of cannabis use disorder is relatively small.

Pharmacological interventions

The review by Copeland (2004) cites a number of studies featuring pharmacological interventions including sustained release bupropion (Haney *et al.* 2001), nefazodone (Haney *et al.* 2003), cannabinoid receptor antagonists (Huestis *et al.* 2001) and agonists (Haney *et al.* 2004; Hart *et al.* 2002). However, all of these involved adult cannabis users who were not actively seeking treatment for drug-related problems. Sustained release bupropion has been used in the treatment of nicotine dependence, and its effects on marijuana withdrawal symptoms were examined by Haney *et al.* (2001) among a group of 10 marijuana smokers. Bupropion was found to have few behavioural effects during the first four days of the study when participants smoked marijuana five times a day. However, during the subsequent 13-day phase of 'placebo' smoking (no delta-9-tetrahydrocannabinol content), symptoms such as irritability, restlessness, depression and sleep disturbance were increased following the administration of bupropion compared with placebo medication. Haney *et al.* (2003) assessed the effects of nefazodone on cannabis withdrawal among seven adults. During an eight-day period of placebo smoking, nefazodone decreased participant ratings of some symptoms, including feeling 'anxious' and 'muscle pain', but had no effect on ratings of feeling 'irritable', 'miserable', or decreased sleep quality. Huestis *et al.* (2001) found that single oral doses of SR141716, a CB1 selective cannabinoid receptor antagonist, resulted in a significant blockade of the psychological and physiological effects of smoked cannabis among a group of 63 adult males. For example, the 90mg dose of the antagonist produced reductions in visual analog ratings of 'how high do you feel now?', 'how stoned are you on marijuana now?' and 'how strong is the drug effect you feel now?' of between 38 and 43%, and a reduction in heart rate of 59%. With regard to the use of cannabinoid agonists, Hart *et al.* (2002) examined the effects of varying doses of oral delta-9-tetrahydrocannabinol (THC) on the choice to self-administer marijuana (smoke a cigarette) in a residential study of 12 healthy research volunteers. Compared with placebo THC, the choice to self-administer was not significantly altered by the administration of oral THC. However, a study of seven adults by Haney *et al.* (2004) found that oral THC did lead to a reduction in marijuana cravings and withdrawal symptoms, compared with placebo, during a placebo smoking phase. The reductions in symptoms included ratings of 'anxious', 'miserable', 'trouble sleeping' and 'chills'. In a second study reported in the same paper, the administration of divalproex, a mood stabiliser, was found to decrease marijuana craving during placebo smoking, but also to increase ratings of 'anxious', 'irritable', 'bad effect' and 'tired'.

Psychological interventions

Zimmermann *et al.* (2004) reviewed the literature on the psychotherapeutic treatment of cannabis abuse and dependence. The authors conducted a systematic search of a number of medical and psychological databases, including Web of Science, Medline and Psycinfo, which was supplemented by a manual retrieval strategy involving the latest issues of relevant journals from 2003 and 2004. The inclusion criteria were clinical trials of treatments for cannabis use disorders using psychotherapeutic intervention strategies and a controlled or randomised controlled study design with pre- and post-treatment measurements. Exclusion criteria were non-specific drug interventions that included cannabis treatments but were not targeted specifically at cannabis use disorder, preventive interventions, self-help approaches for cannabis disorders, pharmacological interventions, and cannabis disorder-specific interventions for special target groups such as particular ethnic groups or patients with mental health disorders. Eight studies met the inclusion criteria and two of these (Dennis *et al.* 2004; Godley *et al.* 2004) featured adolescent participants.

Dennis *et al.* (2004) reported the findings of the Cannabis Youth Treatment Study (CYT), which evaluated the following five outpatient interventions for adolescents with cannabis use disorders:

1. A six-week intervention comprising two sessions of individual motivational enhancement therapy and three weekly sessions of group cognitive behavioural therapy (MET/CBT5).

2. The same intervention but with an additional seven sessions of group cognitive behavioural therapy (MET/CBT12).

3. MET/CBT12, with an additional Family Support Network that included parent education, family therapy and case management over 20 sessions (FSN).

4. 12 weeks of a 14-session intervention based on an Adolescent Community Reinforcement Approach that assists the young person and their family in reshaping their environment, involving ten sessions with the individual and four with care-givers (ACRA).

5. 12 to 15 sessions of a Multidimensional Family Therapy intervention with additional phone and case management contacts over 12 weeks (MDFT).

Participants were 600 adolescents, aged 12 to 18 years, and their families, who were recruited at four treatment sites in the states of Connecticut, Florida, Illinois and Pennsylvania, US. Adolescents were eligible for inclusion if they reported one or more self-reported DSM-IV (APA 1994) criteria for cannabis abuse or dependence, had used cannabis in the past 90 days (or during the 90 days prior to being sent to a controlled environment), and were considered appropriate for outpatient treatment according to American Society of Addiction Medicine criteria (ASAM 1996). Those with other substance use diagnoses and co-occurring psychiatric disorders were also eligible, provided that they could be managed at the outpatient level. Owing to case flow and resource limitations, participants were randomly assigned within each treatment site to one of three conditions, with all five interventions evaluated across two trials (Trial 1 – MET/CBT5 vs. MET/CBT12 vs. FSN; Trial 2 – MET/CBT5 vs. ACRA vs. MDFT).

Across all sites and interventions, the rate of abstinence from all drugs increased from 52 days in the three-month period prior to randomisation to an average of 65 days per quarter across the 12-month follow-up phase. The proportion of participants in recovery (defined as living in the community and reporting no substance use, abuse or dependence in the previous month at the follow-up interview) increased from 3% at the start of the study to an average of 24% across the follow-up period. However, half the adolescents went in and out of periods of recovery and relapse one or more times during the follow-up period, and two-thirds were still reporting substance use or related problems at the 12-month follow-up. There were no significant differences between the five interventions in terms of the total number of days abstinent from all drugs, after controlling for the effects of treatment site and rate of abstinence at the start of the study. Similarly, differences between the interventions in the percentage of adolescents in recovery were not significant, after controlling for treatment site and recovery status in the month before the study. However, when the costs of each intervention were combined with clinical outcomes to estimate the cost per day of abstinence and cost per person in recovery during follow-up, there were a number of significant differences between the interventions. In Trial 1, the MET/CBT5 intervention, and to a lesser extent MET/CBT12, were more cost-effective than FSN, and in Trial 2, ACRA, and to a lesser extent MET/CBT5, were more cost-effective than MDFT.

Godley *et al.* (2004) compared the CYT interventions with the Chestnut Health System's best-practice Outpatient Treatment (CHS) using a quasi-experimental research design. The participants were 274 adolescents admitted to either intervention programme in the state of Illinois, US. The CYT arm of the study included three of the five interventions (MET/CBT5, ACRA, and MDFT) reported by Dennis *et al.* (2004). The CHS programme consisted of individual and family components, with cognitive behavioural, skill, knowledge-based and counselling group sessions being the primary mode of treatment (Godley *et al.* 2003). Participants were assessed at the start of the study and again after 3, 6, 9 and 12 months on a number of variables including substance use, substance-related problems and recovery environment risk. High scores on the latter measure indicate less involvement with support groups and more alcohol and drug use in the home, violent arguments, and physical, emotional and sexual abuse.

After controlling for the effects of demographic and clinical differences at the beginning of the study, the data analyses showed that most of the outcome measures, including levels of substance use and substance-related problems, decreased significantly for participants in both interventions over the course of the 12-month follow-up period. However, changes in some of the outcomes did differ between the interventions. The decrease in substance use was greater for those receiving the CYT

intervention. While the recovery environment risk and level of attendance at self-help meetings remained about the same for the CYT group
throughout the follow-up period, those in the CHS intervention showed
a significant decrease in recovery environment risk and significantly
higher attendance at self-help meetings. The major limitation of this
study acknowledged by the authors was its quasi-experimental design,
which allowed for a number of alternative explanations of the results
other than the treatments themselves (e.g. site differences, history or
sample selection).

The review of cannabis disorder treatments by Copeland (2004) cites
two additional psychological interventions (McCambridge and Strang
2004b; Waldron *et al.* 2001) that were not developed specifically for
cannabis but contained relevant outcomes. McCambridge and Strang
(2004b) reported the findings of a cluster-randomised trial comparing a
single, one-hour session of motivational interviewing that discussed
alcohol, tobacco and illicit drug use with an 'education-as-usual' control
condition. The participants were 200 16- to 20-year-olds from ten
further education colleges in inner London, who were recruited by peers
trained for the study. A group of participants recruited by each peer interviewer represented one cluster, which was then randomised to one of the
two conditions. Outcome measures included changes in self-reported
drug use and motivation to change drug use, which were assessed at the
time of recruitment and again three months later. Participants who
received the motivational interview showed a significant reduction in
cannabis use over the three months, from a mean frequency of 15.7 times
a week at baseline to 5.4 times at follow-up. Cannabis use in the control
group increased from 13.3 times a week to 16.9 times during the same
period. The effect of the intervention on cannabis use was greater among
more frequent users of the drug. Those receiving the intervention were
also three and a half times more likely to have made the decision to stop
or cut down on their use of cannabis than control group participants
during the follow-up period. There were also significant differences in
terms of future intentions of drug use, with 45% of the intervention
group stating at the three-month follow-up that they would not be using
the drug 12 months later, compared with 15% of the control group.

Waldron *et al.* (2001) evaluated the effects of cognitive behavioural therapy (CBT), family therapy, combined individual and family therapy, and a psychoeducational group intervention among 120 13- to 17-year-olds from New Mexico, US, who had been referred for drug abuse treatment. Participants were randomly assigned to one of the four interventions and follow-up assessments were conducted after four and seven months. The principal outcome measures were the percentage of days on which marijuana was used in the 90 days prior to each assessment and the percentage of the sample reporting minimal use, defined as use of the drug on fewer than 10% of the days during this period. Data analyses involved 114 of the original sample who completed both follow-up assessments. Two of the groups, the family and combined family/CBT interventions, showed significant reductions in the percentage of days of marijuana use from pre-treatment to four-month follow-up. During this period, the percentage of youths reporting minimal use showed a significant increase for the family, CBT, and combined family/CBT groups. From pre-treatment to seven-month follow-up, there were significant reductions in the percentage of days of marijuana use for the combined family/CBT and psychoeducational group interventions, and significant increases in minimum use levels for the family, combined family/CBT, and psychoeducational group interventions.

Copeland (2004) also provides details of two interventions that are in the process of being assessed in randomised controlled trials. The Teen Marijuana Check Up in the US (Berghuis *et al.* 2005) and the Adolescent Cannabis Check Up in Australia (Swift, Copeland and Howard 2001) both use a motivational interviewing approach. In the first session, a personalised feedback report is produced for the participant, based on information they provide about their use of drugs, perceptions of the consequences, life goals and readiness to change their drug use. This feedback report is then reviewed with the participant a week later and compared with the patterns of substance use found among their peer group.

Treatment of comorbid conditions

Among the sample of 600 participants in the CYT study, over 95% reported one or more psychological problems other than cannabis use disorders and 84% had three or more problems (Dennis *et al.* 2004).

These included alcohol use disorders (37% of the sample), other sub-stance use disorders (12%), major depression (18%), generalised anxiety (23%), suicidal thoughts (9%) or actions, and traumatic stress disorders (14%), conduct disorder (53%) and attention deficit hyperactivity disorder (38%).

The review by Copeland (2004), however, notes that there have been few studies of interventions among psychiatric populations. Three examples were cited but all involved only adult participants and one did not report cannabis outcomes (Carey *et al.* 2002). The study by Baker *et al.* (2002) featured a sample of 160 patients in an acute psychiatric hospital who were diagnosed with comorbid substance use disorder. Patients were randomly assigned to receive either a brief (30 to 45 minutes) motiva-tional interviewing intervention or a self-help booklet as the control con-dition. Although cannabis use for the sample as a whole decreased signif-icantly from the start of the study to the three-month follow-up, there were no significant differences between the two groups. The study by Green *et al.* (2003) involved a retrospective study of patients who were diagnosed with schizophrenia or schizoaffective disorder and comorbid alcohol and/or cannabis use disorder, and had been treated with either clozapine or risperidone for at least a year. Abstinence from alcohol or cannabis during this period was significantly higher among 33 patients who had been treated with clozapine (54%), compared with eight patients treated with risperidone (13%).

Predictors of relapse during treatment and treatment completion

White *et al.* (2004) assessed possible predictors of relapse while in treat-ment and the completion of treatment among adolescents in an intensive outpatient substance abuse treatment programme in North Carolina, US. Data were extracted from the files of 59 patients who had a primary diag-nosis of marijuana dependence but no other substance dependence, apart from nicotine. The data were coded dichotomously to create a number of variables, including ethnicity, DSM-IV Axis 1 diagnoses (APA 1994), age at first use of marijuana, parental substance abuse history, relapse during treatment (defined as marijuana use while in treatment as detected in a random drug screen), treatment completion and other substance use disorders.

Forty-one of the 59 patients relapsed during treatment. Patients with a diagnosis of depression were significantly more likely to relapse and did so more often than those without the diagnosis. Just over half (52%) of patients with depression were being treated off-site with antidepressant medication. However, the likelihood of relapse and the total number of relapses for these patients were not significantly different from those not receiving this medication. Twenty-nine out of the 59 patients failed to complete the treatment programme. Relapsing while in treatment, a diagnosis of attention deficit hyperactivity disorder, and a maternal history of substance abuse were all associated with a lower likelihood of treatment completion.

Summary

A meta-analysis of universal school-based prevention interventions found that programme type and sample size were significant predictors of programme effectiveness with regard to cannabis use. Interactive programmes that emphasised interpersonal competence and the acquisition of drug refusal skills, with the programme leader in the role of a facilitator rather than teacher, were associated with greater reductions in cannabis use than non-interactive programmes. Larger implementations of both programme types were less effective than smaller ones. One recent example of an interactive intervention which shows some promise is the "Refuse to Use" CD-ROM. Other programmes, such as the Gatehouse Project, have sought to combine both individual and school-level components to address wider issues of student well-being but have so far demonstrated only modest successes. The addition of a community component to a school-based programme appears to be beneficial, as do televised public service announcements designed specifically for adolescents high in sensation seeking.

There is a paucity of research on treatments for cannabis-related problems. A small number of pharmacological interventions have been studied, including sustained release bupropion, nefazodone, selective cannabinoid receptor antagonist and agonists, and divalproex. However, all these involved adult cannabis users who were not actively seeking treatment for drug-related problems. Relatively few randomised controlled trials have been conducted assessing the effectiveness of psychological interventions. Studies have featured a variety of therapies including behavioural, cognitive behavioural, family, motivational and psychoeducational interventions. All the interventions assessed in the CYT study showed positive effects on clinical outcomes, although there were some differences in terms of cost-effectiveness.

Many cannabis users presenting for treatment are characterised by a number of comorbid problems, but there have been few studies of interventions among psychiatric populations. The importance of addressing this issue is underlined by the results of a study examining predictors of relapse and treatment completion, which found that patients with a diagnosis of depression were more likely to relapse and did so more often, and a diagnosis of attention deficit hyperactivity disorder predicted a lower likelihood of completing treatment.

8 Cannabis Policy

The legal status of cannabis

Cannabis is classified as a narcotic drug under Schedules I and IV of the 1961 United Nations (UN) Single Convention on Narcotic Drugs (EMCDDA 2004b). International controls on cannabis date from a decision made at the 1924–25 League of Nations' Second Opium Conference in Geneva, Switzerland (Kendell 2003). Although the drug was not on the conference agenda, the Egyptian delegation claimed that cannabis, or Indian hemp as it was known at the time, was as dangerous as opium and should therefore be included on the list of narcotics subject to legislative controls. It was described as being highly addictive and leading to various forms of physical and intellectual decline, including insanity.

Countries that are signatories to the UN convention are required to ensure that drug-related activities such as production, cultivation and possession are punishable by law. However, they are able to apply their law according to their own particular circumstances. Since the 1970s, a number of US states, parts of Australia and several countries in Europe, most notably in the case of the Netherlands, have liberalised their laws governing cannabis to varying degrees. Supporters of liberalisation argue that criminal convictions for cannabis possession and use are out of all proportion to the nature of the offence, and can have a significant negative impact on the lives of those who are convicted, not just in terms of fines or imprisonment but also on family relations and employment prospects (Single, Christie and Ali 2000). Prohibitive legislation also makes it difficult for young people to obtain information about the concentration or purity of the cannabis they use and less harmful ways of using it, and buying the drug on the black market can often bring them into contact with dealers of other illicit substances (Wodak *et al.* 2002).

In a review of the evidence base for harm reduction approaches in substance use, Hunt (2005) describes the range of policy options that come under the general term of 'depenalisation' or 'decriminalisation'. This is defined as the 'removal of penal controls and criminal sanctions in relation to an activity, which however remains prohibited and subject to non-penal regulations and sanctions' (UN ODCCP 2000, p18). 'De jure' depenalisation involves actual changes in the laws governing particular substances. One example is partial prohibition, where personal use is permitted but commercial activities remain illegal. With 'de facto' depenalisation, drug use remains illegal but the way in which the law is applied is altered, such as the use of cautioning rather than formal charging and prosecution, particularly in cases involving small quantities of the drug for personal use.

Policy impact studies

Australia

A number of states and territories in Australia have introduced changes in the laws governing the use and possession of cannabis (Single *et al.* 2000). In 1987, South Australia implemented the Cannabis Expiation Notice (CEN) scheme, whereby it was no longer a criminal offence to possess small quantities of the drug (less than 100 grams or 20 grams in the case of cannabis resin) for personal use. Individuals would instead be issued with an infringement notice, which could be expiated following the payment of a fine. The Australian Capital Territory and the Northern Territory introduced similar schemes during the 1990s. In 1998, the state of Victoria implemented a system of cautions for minor cannabis offenders, a similar form of which was later introduced by Western Australia.

Donnelly, Hall and Christie (2000) examined the impact of the CEN scheme by comparing levels of lifetime and weekly cannabis use in South Australia with those in other parts of the country. The data were collected as part of five National Drug Strategy household surveys of the general population, aged 14 years and over, covering the period from 1985 to

1995. The surveys showed that the proportion of respondents in South Australia who had used cannabis increased from 25.7% in 1985 to 36.3% in 1995. However, there were also significant increases during this time in states where there had been no change in the drug's legal status, such as Tasmania (21.1 to 32.9%), and Victoria (26.4 to 32%). The rate of increase in lifetime use in South Australia was significantly greater than the average increase for the rest of the country, although there were no differences in the rates of change between South Australia, Tasmania and Victoria. New South Wales, Queensland and Western Australia had lower rates of increase than South Australia, while lifetime use in the Northern Territory and the Australian Capital Territory did not show a significant change over the ten years. Weekly cannabis use in South Australia rose from 2.9% in 1988 to 7% in 1991, although Donnelly *et al.* (2000) commented that the significance of this change was questionable, as the 1988 sample comprised only 193 respondents. Furthermore, the rate of weekly use subsequently declined to 6.5% in 1993 and 4.9% in 1995. There was also a sharp increase in weekly cannabis use in Tasmania between 1991 (1.6%) and 1993 (5.3%). However, none of the other states or territories in the country showed any significant changes in weekly use between 1988 and 1995, and there was no significant difference between South Australia and the rest of the country in terms of the rate of increase.

In their review of the impact of decriminalisation in Australia, Single *et al.* (2000) cite an additional study by Ali *et al.* (1999), which found that neither the CEN scheme of South Australia nor the more prohibitive drug laws of Western Australia had much of an effect on people's future intentions to use cannabis. Most cannabis offenders stated that the possibility of receiving another expiation notice or conviction would not deter them from using the drug again.

The US

Between 1973 and 1978, 11 states introduced legislation that reduced the maximum penalties for cannabis possession to a fine. Single *et al.* (2000) cite a number of studies evaluating the effects of these changes in the states of Oregon (Drug Abuse Council 1974–1977), Maine (Maine Office of Alcoholism and Drug Abuse Prevention 1979), Ohio (Spitzner 1979) and California (Budman 1977). The general pattern of findings was one of a modest increase in the rate of cannabis use following the decriminalisation measures. However, the Oregon and Maine studies did not collect prospective data on cannabis use prior to the introduction of the measures. Furthermore, none of the four evaluations featured a controlled comparison with other areas maintaining a more prohibitive drug policy. An analysis of data from four national surveys conducted between 1972 and 1977 found that while marijuana use had increased in states that had changed their drug laws, levels of use had risen even more in those states with the most severe legal penalties (Saveland and Bray 1980).

In their discussion of various topics related to the legalisation of marijuana, Joffe and Yancy (2004) cite two additional studies assessing the impact of decriminalisation. Johnston, O'Malley and Bachman (1981) analysed data from the Monitoring the Future surveys of high school students, conducted between 1975 and 1980, and concluded that decriminalisation had had no effect on the students' use of the drug. However, an analysis of the 1992–1994 surveys found greater and more frequent levels of marijuana use among young people who lived in decriminalised states (Chaloupka et al. 1999).

Single et al. (2000) suggest that trends in cannabis use may have more to do with changes in perceptions of the health risks associated with the drug than changes in its legal status. Findings from the US National Household Survey on Drug Abuse show an increase in the perceived health risks of cannabis use between 1985 and 1990, during which time the proportion of 12- to 17-year-olds reporting cannabis use in the past month was decreasing. However, a decline in perceived health risks from 1993 onwards was accompanied by a rise in the reports of cannabis use.

The Netherlands

In 1976, the Netherlands adopted a system of 'de facto' decriminalisation of cannabis. Although possession of the drug remained illegal, the policy of the Dutch Ministry of Justice was non-enforcement of the law in cases involving possession or sale of up to 30 grams. This threshold was lowered to 5 grams in 1995. The purchase of small quantities of the drug by adults is allowed in commercial establishments known as 'coffee shops' according to a set of guidelines. These include no advertising of cannabis, no sales to minors and no sale of other illicit 'hard' drugs (e.g. cocaine).

MacCoun and Reuter (2001) examined the impact of these policies on the levels of lifetime cannabis use among adolescents and young adults, using data from a number of sources covering the period from 1970 to 1996. They concluded that cannabis use in the Netherlands was already declining among adolescents prior to 1976 and that decriminalisation had little effect on levels of use during the late 1970s and early 1980s. However, the proportion of 18- to 20-year-olds who had used cannabis rose from 15% in 1984 to 44% by 1996 and reports of use in the previous month increased from 8.5% to 18.5%. MacCoun and Reuter (2001) hypothesised that this increase in cannabis use was the result of a progression from a 'passive' depenalisation policy to 'de facto' legalisation, characterised by the emergence of the 'coffee shops' and a growing 'commercialisation' of the drug.

Korf (2002) noted that the trends in cannabis use in the Netherlands over the last three decades appear to run parallel to changes in the availability of cannabis and cannabis policy during this period. The first peak in the use of cannabis, around 1970, occurred at a time when the drug's retail market was primarily an 'underground' one and part of a general youth counterculture. The number of users decreased during the 1970s with the emergence of a more limited number of 'house dealers'. Prevalence rose again from the mid-1980s onwards with the establishment of the more accessible 'coffee shops'. Rates stabilised but then started to decrease slightly by the middle of the 1990s at around the time when local communities were given the power to decide whether they wanted coffee shops in their area, and when the minimum age for customers was raised from 16 to 18.

To shed further light on the impact of decriminalisation, MacCoun and Reuter (2001) compared the prevalence of cannabis use in the Netherlands with the US and other European countries. The selection criteria for the comparisons were cross-sectional surveys that were matched for survey year, measure of prevalence (lifetime, past year or past month use) and age groups covered. A total of 28 comparisons met these criteria.

Four comparisons involved national estimates of lifetime use in the Netherlands and the US. Three of these comparisons showed only slight differences in prevalence (2% or less) between the countries, but one revealed a lifetime use rate of 32.9% in the US compared with 15.6% in the Netherlands. Twelve comparisons involved US national data and a single Dutch city (Amsterdam, Utrecht or Tilburg). US prevalence rates were broadly similar to those in Amsterdam and Utrecht (average differences in prevalence of less than 2%), but higher than those reported in Tilburg (average difference of 7.9%). Twelve comparisons were made between the Netherlands and six other European countries, although seven of these compared the rates of one country as a whole with the largest city in the other. On average, Dutch prevalence rates were around 5% higher than the comparison European countries or cities. However, much of this higher prevalence was attributable to the comparisons involving Amsterdam. Furthermore, figures from the 1995–96 European School Project on Alcohol and Drug Use survey (ESPAD), which uses a standardised survey methodology, noted that lifetime use among 15- to 16-year-olds was substantially lower in the Netherlands (29.3%) than in the UK (41%).

MacCoun and Reuter (2001) also compared the trends in cannabis use over time for the Netherlands, the US and Oslo, Norway. During the period from 1984 to 1992, when cannabis use was increasing in the Netherlands, prevalence rates among high school senior students in the US were declining and the levels of use among 15- to 21-year-olds in Oslo were relatively stable. However, cannabis use in all three cases increased between 1992 and 1996.

Abraham, Cohen and Beukenhorst (2001) have criticised the MacCoun and Reuter (2001) analyses, noting that the 16 comparisons involving a Dutch city with an entire nation presuppose that prevalence rates are the same all over the Netherlands. They refer to the findings of a national survey of licit and illicit drug use conducted in 1997 (Abraham, Cohen and van Til 1999), which found that lifetime prevalence in Amsterdam was 36.7%, prevalence for the Netherlands as a whole was 15.6% and for rural areas 10.5%. De Zwart and van Laar (2001) have also commented that some of the analyses compared the results of school surveys, which typically record higher levels of substance prevalence, with those of general population surveys.

A more recent study assessing the relationship between different drug policies and cannabis use compared Amsterdam with San Francisco (Reinarman, Cohen and Kaal 2004). These cities were chosen specifically because of their similarities on a range of demographic and cultural characteristics. Participants in both cities were recruited from drug prevalence surveys of the general population. Respondents who were classified as 'experienced users' (defined as using the drug 25 or more times during their lives) were invited to take part in an interview to gather further details about their cannabis use. A total of 216 out of 535 experienced users in the Amsterdam sample were interviewed, with 266 out of 349 agreeing to participate in San Francisco. Respondents were compared on a number of aspects relating to cannabis use, including age at onset of use and the frequency and quantity of use. To assess changes over time, respondents were asked about their experiences in four time periods: the first year of regular use (defined as use of the drug once a month or more), the period of maximum use, use in the past year, and use in the past three months.

The findings indicated that, despite the differences in the drug policies between the cities, there were strong similarities in the experiences of the two groups of cannabis users. The mean age at onset of cannabis use was 16.95 years in Amsterdam and 16.43 in San Francisco. The overall pattern of reported marijuana use was similar across both cities, although Amsterdam respondents reported significantly more frequent use (once a week or more) than did San Francisco users during their first year of regular use and period of maximum use. In the first year of regular use, few respondents in either city used large quantities of cannabis, with only 3% in Amsterdam and 5% in San Francisco consuming 28 grams (approximately an ounce) during an average month of use. However, Amsterdam respondents used significantly smaller quantities than did San Francisco respondents during the first year of regular use. Larger quantities of the drug were consumed during the periods of maximum use, but levels were again very similar in Amsterdam and San Francisco. In each city, 18% of respondents used an average of 28 grams or more per month during the maximum use phase.

The most common 'career' use pattern or trajectory of use in both cities was a gradual increase in use followed by sustained decline (49.4% of the total sample from both cities). However, a pattern of stable use was more common among Amsterdam respondents (11.1%) than San Francisco users (1.9%), whereas intermittent use was more likely in San Francisco (9.5%) than in Amsterdam (3.2%). With regard to the use of other illicit drugs, there was a significantly lower lifetime prevalence of cocaine, crack, amphetamine, ecstasy and opiate use in Amsterdam than in San Francisco. During the three months prior to the interview, levels of crack and opiate use were also significantly lower in Amsterdam than in San Francisco.

Summary

Although signatories to the UN convention on narcotics are required to ensure that drug-related activities are punishable by law, a number of countries have introduced changes to the way they apply their laws governing cannabis. A number of different types of 'decriminalisation' have been implemented, such as the Cannabis Expiation Notice Scheme in South Australia and the establishment of the 'coffee shops' in the Netherlands. A rise in cannabis use was recorded following the introduction of the CEN scheme, but increases were also noted in other parts of Australia where the drug's legal status was unchanged. Impact studies conducted in the US show mixed findings, although some have a number of methodological limitations. Comparisons of the Dutch experience of decriminalisation with other countries do not show any consistent relationship between the prevalence of cannabis and the drug's legal status. Some countries with more prohibitive drug laws than the Netherlands have lower levels of use, while others report higher rates. The use of cannabis has developed in a wave-like pattern in a number of countries and may have more to do with young people's attitude to the drug itself (e.g. perceptions of the health risks) than current cannabis policy.

9 Concluding Comments

The latest available data from the Health Behaviour in School-aged Children study, which includes samples from Europe and North America, show that among 15-year-olds, around a fifth of females and a quarter of males have tried cannabis at least once in their lives. The findings from a number of longitudinal cohort studies show that a significant proportion of those who experiment with the drug continue to use at some level during adolescence. Furthermore, UK research indicates that prevalence is considerably higher among particular groups such as pupils expelled or suspended from school, the young homeless and young offenders. The use of cannabis is associated with an increased risk of a range of psychosocial problems. Although the relationship between these variables is attributable, to varying degrees, to the effects of other factors and a non-causal explanation remains a possibility, the findings underline the importance of continued prevention strategies to minimise any of these potential effects.

Preventive interventions need to acknowledge that the way in which young people view cannabis is often quite different from their perception of other illicit substances. Studies examining the perceived functions of drug use have provided a valuable insight into the reasons why adolescents use cannabis and the findings can be used to guide the content of future preventive strategies. For example, programmes could focus on alternative means of achieving the same functions that individuals cite for their use of the drug.

Preventive programmes also need to address the relationships between the use of cannabis and tobacco. Longitudinal cohort studies have identified smoking as one of the main predictors of later cannabis use in adolescence, and a number of qualitative studies have also found that the use of cannabis can reinforce smoking and make it difficult for young people to quit the habit. The reduction of cannabis use should therefore be seen as part of a wider strategy to reduce teenage smoking. The need for a coordinated campaign against the two substances has recently been acknowledged in the 'Fags and Hash' conference organised by the Scottish Tobacco Control Alliance in April 2005 (BBC 2005c).

Research indicates that a small percentage of users will meet the criteria for substance dependence and require appropriate treatment. However, there is a paucity of research on both pharmacological and psychological interventions. This is an area that requires further attention, particularly with regard to the treatment of comorbid conditions, which characterise many cannabis users.

Resources

Add Health – The National Longitudinal Study of Adolescent Health
www.cpc.unc.edu/projects/addhealth

Christchurch Health and Development Study
www.chmeds.ac.nz/research/chds

Cochrane Library
www.nelh.nhs.uk/cochrane.asp

DrugScope
www.drugscope.org.uk

Dunedin Multidisciplinary Health and Development Study
http://dunedinstudy.otago.ac.nz

European School Survey Project on Alcohol and Other Drugs (ESPAD)
www.espad.org

European Monitoring Centre for Drugs and Drug Addiction (EMCDDA)
www.emcdda.eu.int

Health Behaviour in School-aged Children Study (HBSC)
www.hbsc.org

Tackling Drugs Changing Lives
www.drugs.gov.uk

Talk to Frank
www.talktofrank.com

UK Home Office – drugs website
www.homeoffice.gov.uk/drugs

References

Abraham, M., Cohen, P. Beukenhorst, D., and de Winter, M. (2001) 'Comparative cannabis use data.' *British Journal of Psychiatry 179,* 175–177.

Abraham, M., Cohen, P. and van Til, R. (1999) *Licit and Illicit Drug Use in the Netherlands.* Amsterdam: Centre for Drug Research (CEDRO).

AIHW (Australian Institute of Health and Welfare) (2003) *Alcohol and Other Drug Treatment Services in Australia: Findings from the National Minimum Data Set 2001–02. 16 Bulletin No. 10.* AIHW cat. no. AUS 40 (pp.1–2). Canberra: AIHW.

Ali, R., Christie, P., Lenton, S., Hawks, D., Sutton, A., Hall, W. and Allsop, S. (1999) *The Social Impacts of the Cannabis Expiation Notice Scheme in South Australia.* Canberra: Department of Health and Aged Care.

Amos, A., Wiltshire, S., Bostock, Y., Haw, S. and McNeill, A. (2004) '"You can't go without a fag…you need it for your hash" – a qualitative exploration of smoking, cannabis and young people.' *Addiction 99,* 77–81.

Andreasson, S., Allebeck, P., Engstrom, A. and Rydberg, U. (1987) 'Cannabis and schizophrenia: a longitudinal study of Swedish conscripts.' *Lancet ii,* 1483–1486.

APA (American Psychiatric Association) (1987) *Diagnostic and Statistical Manual of Mental Disorders: DSM-III-R.* 3rd edn., revised. Washington, DC: APA.

APA (1994) *Diagnostic and Statistical Manual of Mental Disorders: DSM-IV.* 4th edn. Washington, DC: APA.

APA (2000) *Diagnostic and Statistical Manual of Mental Disorders: DSM-IV.* 4th edn., revised. Washington, DC: APA.

Arseneault, L., Cannon, M., Poulton, R., Murray, R., Caspi, A. and Moffitt, T. (2002) 'Cannabis use in adolescence and risk for adult psychosis: longitudinal prospective study.' *British Medical Journal 325,* 1212–1213.

Arseneault, L., Cannon, M., Witton, J. and Murray, R. (2004) 'Causal association between cannabis and psychosis: examination of the evidence.' *British Journal of Psychiatry 184,* 110–117.

ASAM (American Society of Addiction Medicine) (1996) *Patient Placement Criteria for the Treatment of Psychoactive Substance Disorders.* 2nd edn. Chevy Chase, MD: ASAM.

Ashton, C. (2001) 'Pharmacology and effects of cannabis: a brief review.' *British Journal of Psychiatry 178,* 101–106.

Bailey, S., Flewelling, R. and Rachal, J. (1992) 'Predicting continued use of marijuana among adolescents: the relative influence of drug-specific and social context factors.' *Journal of Health and Social Behavior 33,* 51–66.

Bailey, S. and Hubbard, R. (1990) 'Developmental variation in the context of marijuana initiation among adolescents.' *Journal of Health and Social Behaviour 31,* 58–70.

95

Baker, A., Lewin, T., Reichler, H., Clancy, R., Carr, V., Garrett, R., Sly, K., Devir, H. and Terry, M. (2002) 'Evaluation of a motivational interview for substance use within psychiatric in-patient services.' *Addiction 97*, 1329–1337.

Bardone, A., Moffitt, T., Caspi, A., Dickson, N., Stanton, W. and Silva, P. (1998) 'Adult physical health outcomes of adolescent girls with conduct disorder, depression, and anxiety.' *Journal of the American Academy of Child and Adolescent Psychiatry 37*, 594–601.

BBC (2005a) 'Clarke orders rethink on cannabis.' Saturday 19 March, 2005. http://news.bbc.co.uk/1/hi/uk/4364625.stm

BBC (2005b) 'GPs "should address cannabis use".' Tuesday 18 January, 2005. http://news.bbc.co.uk/1/hi/health/4182419.stm

BBC (2005c) '"Fags and hash" fears for health.' Thursday 21 April, 2005. http://news.bbc.co.uk/1/hi/scotland/4465621.stm

Bell, R., Pavis, S., Cunningham-Burley, S. and Amos, A. (1998) 'Young men's use of cannabis: exploring changes in meaning and context over time.' *Drugs: Education, Prevention and Policy 5*, 141–155.

Berghuis, J., Swift, W., Roffman, R., Stephens, R. and Copeland, J. (2005: in press). 'The Teen Cannabis Check-Up: exploring strategies for reaching young cannabis users.' In R. Roffman and R. Stephens (eds) *Cannabis Dependence: Its Nature, Consequences and Treatment* New York: Cambridge University Press.

Bond, L., Thomas, L., Coffey, C., Glover, S., Butler, H., Carlin, J. and Patton, G. (2004) 'Long-term impact of the Gatehouse Project on cannabis use of 16-year-olds in Australia.' *Journal of School Health 74*, 23–29.

Boys, A., Farrell, M., Taylor, C., Marsden, J., Goodman, R., Brugha, T., Bebbington, P., Jenkins, R. and Meltzer, H. (2003) 'Psychiatric morbidity and substance use in young people aged 13–15 years: results from the Child and Adolescent Survey of Mental Health.' *British Journal of Psychiatry 182*, 509–517.

Boys, A., Marsden, J., Griffiths, P., Fountain, J., Stillwell, G. and Strang, J. (1999) 'Substance use among young people: the relationship between perceived functions and intentions.' *Addiction 94*, 1043–1050.

Boys, A. and Marsden, J. (2003) 'Perceived functions predict intensity of use and problems in young polysubstance users.' *Addiction 98*, 951–963.

Boys, A., Marsden, J. and Strang, J. (2001) 'Understanding reasons for drug use amongst young people: a functional perspective.' *Health Education Research 16*, 457–469.

Brill, H. and Nahas, G. (1984) 'Cannabis intoxication and mental illness.' In G. Nahas (ed.) *Marihuana in Science and Medicine.* New York: Raven Press.

Brook, J., Brook, D., de la Rosa, M., Duque, L., Rodriguez, E., Montoya, I. and Whiteman, M. (1998) 'Pathways to marijuana use among adolescents: cultural/ecological, family, peer, and personality influences.' *Journal of the American Academy of Child and Adolescent Psychiatry 37*, 759–766.

Brook, J., Cohen, P. and Brook, D. (1998) 'Longitudinal study of co-occurring psychiatric disorders and substance use.' *Journal of the American Academy of Child and Adolescent Psychiatry 37*, 322–330.

Budman, K. (1977) *A First Report of the Impact of California's New Marijuana Law (SB95).* Sacramento, CA: State Office of Narcotics and Drug Abuse.

Carey, K., Carey, M., Maisto, S. and Purnine, D. (2002) 'The feasibility of enhancing psychiatric outpatients' readiness to change their substance use.' *Psychiatric Services 53*, 602–608.

Central Survey Unit (2005) *Young Person's Behaviour and Attitudes Survey Bulletin: October 2003–November 2003.* www.csu.nisra.gov.uk

Chaloupka, F., Pacula, R., Farrelly, M., Johnston, M. and O'Malley, P. (1999) *Do Higher Cigarette Prices Encourage Youth to Use Marijuana?* Working paper 6939. Cambridge, MA: National Bureau of Economic Research.

Chen, C.-Y. and Anthony, J. (2003) 'Possible age-associated bias in reporting of clinical features of drug dependence: epidemiological evidence on adolescent-onset marijuana use.' *Addiction 98*, 71–82.

Christian, J., Crome, I., Gilvarry, E., Johnson, P., McArdle, P. and McCarthy, S. (2001) *The Substance of Young Needs.* London: Health Advisory Service.

Cleghorn, J., Kaplan, R., Szechtman, B., Szechtman, H., Brown, G. and Franco, S. (1991) 'Substance abuse and schizophrenia: effect on symptoms but not on neurocognitive function.' *Journal of Clinical Psychiatry 52*, 26–30.

Coffey, C., Carlin, J., Lynskey, M., Li, N. and Patton, G. (2003) 'Adolescent precursors of cannabis dependence: findings from the Victorian Adolescent Health Cohort Study.' *British Journal of Psychiatry 182*, 330–336.

Coffey, C., Lynskey, M., Wolfe, R. and Patton, G. (2000) 'Initiation and progression of cannabis use in a population-based Australian adolescent longitudinal study.' *Addiction 95*, 1679–1690.

Condon, J. and Smith, N. (2003) *Prevalence of Drug Use: Key Findings from the 2002/2003 British Crime Survey.* London: Home Office.

Copeland, J. (2004) 'Developments in the treatment of cannabis use disorder.' *Current Opinion in Psychiatry 17*, 161–167.

Corbett, J., Akhtar, P., Currie, D. and Currie, C. (2005) *Scottish Schools Adolescent Lifestyle and Substance Use Survey (SALSUS) National Report: Smoking, Drinking and Drug Use among 13 and 15 year olds in Scotland in 2004.* Norwich: The Stationery Office.

Costello, A., Edelbrock, C., Kalas, R., Kessler, M. and Klaric, S. (1982) *Diagnostic Interview Schedule for Children – DISC.* Bethesda, MD: National Institute of Mental Health.

Crowley, T., Macdonald, M., Whitmore, E. and Mikulich, S. (1998) 'Cannabis dependence, withdrawal, and reinforcing effects among adolescents with conduct symptoms and substance use disorders.' *Drug and Alcohol Dependence 50*, 27–37.

Currie, C., Roberts, C., Morgan, A., Smith, R., Settertobulte, W., Samdal, O. and Rasmussen, V. (2004) *Young People's Health in Context: Health Behaviour in School-aged Children (HBSC) Study. International Report from the 2001/2002 Survey.* Copenhagen: World Health Organization.

Degenhardt, L., Hall, W. and Lynskey, M. (2003a) 'Testing hypotheses about the relationship between cannabis use and psychosis.' *Drug and Alcohol Dependence 71*, 37–48.

Degenhardt, L., Hall, W. and Lynskey, M. (2003b) 'Exploring the association between cannabis use and depression.' *Addiction 98*, 1493–1504.

Dennis, M., Godley, S., Diamond, G., Tims, F., Babor, T., Donaldson, J., Liddle, H., Titus, J., Kaminer, Y., Webb, C., Hamilton, N. and Funk, R. (2004) 'The Cannabis Youth Treatment (CYT) Study: main findings from two randomized trials.' *Journal of Substance Abuse Treatment 27*, 197–213.

Department of Health (2005) *Smoking, Drinking and Drug Use among Young People in England 2004: Headline Figures.* www.dh.gov.uk

Derogatis, J. (1983) *SCL-90-R: Administration, Scoring, and Procedures Manual-II.* Towson, MD: Clinical Psychometric Research.

Derogatis, L., Lipman, R. and Covi, L. (1973) 'SCL-90: an outpatient psychiatric rating scale – preliminary report.' *Psychopharmacology 9*, 13–28.

Derzon, J. and Lipsey, M. (1999) 'A synthesis of the relationship of marijuana use with delinquent and problem behaviors.' *School Psychology International 20*, 57–68.

de Zwart, W. and van Laar, M. (2001) 'Cannabis regimes.' *British Journal of Psychiatry 178*, 574.

Dixon, L., Haas, G., Wedien, P., Sweeney, J. and Frances, A. (1990) 'Acute effects of drug abuse in schizophrenic patients: clinical observations and patients' self-reports.' *Schizophrenia Bulletin 16*, 69–79.

Donnelly, N., Hall, W. and Christie, P. (2000) 'The effects of the Cannabis Expiation Notice system on the prevalence of cannabis use in South Australia: evidence from the National Drug Strategy Household Surveys 1985-95.' *Drug and Alcohol Review 19*, 265–269.

Drug Abuse Council (1974–1977) *Marijuana Survey – State of Oregon, News Releases.* Washington, DC: Drug Abuse Council.

Drugscope (2005) 'Cannabis.' www.drugscope.org.uk/druginfo/drugsearch

Duffy, A. and Milin, R. (1996) 'Case study: withdrawal syndrome in adolescent chronic cannabis users.' *Journal of the American Academy of Child and Adolescent Psychiatry 35*, 1618–1621.

Duncan, T., Duncan, S., Beauchamp, N., Wells, J. and Ary, D. (2000) 'Development and evaluation of an interactive CD-ROM refusal skills program to prevent youth substance use: "Refuse to Use".' *Journal of Behavioral Medicine 23*, 59–72.

Ellickson, P., Bui, K., Bell, R. and McGuigan, K. (1998) 'Does early drug use increase the risk of dropping out of high school?' *Journal of Drug Issues 28*, 357–380.

Ellickson, P., Martino, S. and Collins, R. (2004a) 'Marijuana use from adolescence to young adulthood: multiple developmental trajectories and their associated outcomes.' *Health Psychology 23*, 299–307.

Ellickson, P., Tucker, J., Klein, D. and Saner, H. (2004b) 'Antecedents and outcomes of marijuana use initiation during adolescence.' *Preventive Medicine 39*, 976–984.

Elliott, D. and Huizinga, D. (1989) 'Improving self-reported measures in delinquency.' In M. Klein (ed.) *Cross National Research in Self Reported Crime and Delinquency.* Dordrecht: Kluwer Academic Publishers, pp 155–186.

Elliott, D., Huizinga, D. and Ageton, S. (1985) *Explaining Delinquency and Drug Use.* Beverly Hills, CA: Sage Publications.

Elliott, D., Huizinga, D. and Menard, S. (1989) *Multiple Problem Youth: Delinquency, Substance Use and Mental Health Problems.* New York: Springer-Verlag.

ElSohly, M., Ross, S., Mehmedic, Z., Arafat, R., Yi, B. and Banahan, B. (2000) 'Potency trends of delta-9-THC and other cannabinoids in confiscated marijuana from 1980 to 1997.' *Journal of Forensic Science 45*, 24–30.

EMCDDA (European Monitoring Centre for Drugs and Drug Addiction) (2004a) *EMCDDA Insights: An Overview of Cannabis Potency in Europe.* Luxembourg: Office for Official Publications of the European Communities.

EMCDDA (2004b) *Annual Report: The State of the Drugs Problem in the European Union and Norway.* www.emcdda.eu.int

ESPAD (2005) *The European School Survey Project on Alcohol and Other Drugs. Summary of 2003 Findings.* www.espad.org

Fergusson, D. and Horwood, L. (1997) 'Early onset cannabis use and psychosocial adjustment in young adults.' *Addiction 97*, 279–296.

Fergusson, D. and Horwood, L. (2000a) 'Cannabis use and dependence in a New Zealand birth cohort.' *New Zealand Medical Journal 113*, 156–158.

Fergusson, D. and Horwood, L. (2000b) 'Does cannabis use encourage other forms of illicit drug use?' *Addiction 95*, 505–520.

Fergusson, D. and Horwood, L. (2001) 'The Christchurch Health and Development Study: review of findings on child and adolescent mental health.' *Australian and New Zealand Journal of Psychiatry 35*, 287–296.

Fergusson, D., Horwood, L. and Beautrais, A. (2003a) 'Cannabis and educational achievement.' *Addiction 98*, 1681–1692.

Fergusson, D., Horwood, L., Lynskey, M. and Madden, P. (2003b) 'Early reactions to cannabis predict later dependence.' *Archives of General Psychiatry 60*, 1033–1039.

Fergusson, D., Horwood, L. and Ridder, E. (2005) 'Tests of causal linkages between cannabis use and psychotic symptoms.' *Addiction 100*, 354–366.

Fergusson, D., Horwood, L. and Swain-Campbell, N. (2002) 'Cannabis use and psychosocial adjustment in adolescence and young adulthood.' *Addiction 97*, 1123–1135.

Fergusson, D., Horwood, L. and Swain-Campbell, N. (2003c) 'Cannabis dependence and psychotic symptoms in young people.' *Psychological Medicine 33*, 15–21.

Fergusson, D., Lynskey, M. and Horwood, L. (1993) 'Conduct problems and attention deficit behaviour in middle childhood and cannabis use by age 15.' *Australian and New Zealand Journal of Psychiatry 27*, 673–682.

Fergusson, D., Lynskey, M. and Horwood, L. (1996) 'The short-term consequences of early onset cannabis use.' *Journal of Abnormal Child Psychology 24*, 499–512.

Fountain, J., Bartlett, H., Griffiths, P., Gossop, M. Boys, A. and Strang, J. (1999) 'Why say no? Reasons given by young people for not using drugs.' *Addiction Research 7*, 339–353.

Godley, S., Jones, N., Funk, R., Ives, M. and Passetti, L. (2004) 'Comparing outcomes of best-practice and research-based outpatient treatment protocols for adolescents.' *Journal of Psychoactive Drugs 36*, 35–48.

Godley, S., Risberg, R., Adams, L. and Sodetz, A. (2003) 'Chestnut Health System's Bloomington outpatient and intensive outpatient program for adolescent substance abusers.' In S. Stevens and A. Morral (eds) *Adolescent Substance Abuse Treatment in the United States: Exemplary Models from a National Evaluation Study.* Binghampton, NY: Haworth Press, pp 57–80.

Goulden, C. and Sondhi, A. (2001) *At the Margins: Drug Use by Vulnerable Young People in the 1998/99 Youth Lifestyles Survey.* London: Home Office.

Green, A., Burgess, E., Dawson, R., Zimmet, S. and Strous, R. (2003) 'Alcohol and cannabis use in schizophrenia: effects of clozapine vs risperidone.' *Schizophrenia Research 60*, 81–85.

Hall, W. and Degenhardt, L. (2000) 'Cannabis use and psychosis: a review of clinical and epidemiological evidence.' *Australian and New Zealand Journal of Psychiatry 34*, 26–34.

Hall, W., Solowij, N. and Lemon, J. (1994) *The Health and Psychological Consequences of Cannabis Use.* Canberra: Commonwealth Department of Human Services and Health.

Hammersley, R., Marsland, L. and Reid, M. (2003) *Substance Use by Young Offenders: The Impact of the Normalisation of Drug Use in the Early Years of the 21st Century.* London: Home Office.

Haney, M., Hart, C., Vosburg, S., Nasser, J., Bennett, A., Zubaran, C. and Foltin, R. (2004) 'Marijuana withdrawal in humans: effects of oral THC or divalproex.' *Neuropsychopharmacology 29*, 158–170.

Haney, M., Hart, C., Ward, A. and Foltin, R. (2003) 'Nefazodone decreases anxiety during marijuana withdrawal in humans.' *Psychopharmacology 165*, 157–165.

Haney, M., Ward, A., Comer, S., Hart, C., Foltin, R. and Fischman, M. (2001) 'Bupropion SR worsens mood during marijuana withdrawal in humans.' *Psychopharmacology 155*, 171–179.

Hart, C., Haney, M., Ward, A., Fischman, M. and Foltin, R. (2002) 'Effects of oral THC maintenance on smoked marijuana self-administration.' *Drug and Alcohol Dependence 67*, 301–309.

Henquet, C., Krabbendam, L., Spauwen, J., Kaplan, C., Lieb, R., Wittchen, H-U. and van Os, J. (2005) 'Prospective cohort study of cannabis use, predisposition for psychosis, and psychotic symptoms in young people.' *British Medical Journal 330*, 11–14.

Highet, G. (2004) 'The role of cannabis in supporting young people's cigarette smoking: a qualitative exploration.' *Health Education Research 19*, 635–643.

Hofstra, M., van der Ende, J. and Verhultz, F. (2002) 'Child and adolescent problems predict DSM-IV disorders in adulthood: a 14-year follow-up of a Dutch epidemiological sample.' *Journal of the American Academy of Child and Adolescent Psychiatry 41*, 182–189.

Home Office (2005) 'Cannabis reclassification.' www.homeoffice.gov.uk/drugs-laws/cannabis-reclassifications

Huestis, M., Gorelick, D., Heishman, S., Preston, K., Nelson, R., Moolchan, E. and Frank, R. (2001) 'Blockade of effects of smoked marijuana by the CB1-selective cannabinoid receptor antagonist SR141716.' *Archives of General Psychiatry 58*, 322–328.

Hunt, N. (2005) 'A review of the evidence-base for harm reduction approaches to drug use.' www.forward-thinking-on-drugs.org/review2-print.hmtl

IDMU (Independent Drug Monitoring Unit) (2005) 'History of cannabis: how cannabis was criminalised.' www.idmu.co.uk/historical.htm

Jablensky, A., Sartorius, N., Emberg, G., Anker, M., Korten, A., Cooper, J. *et al.* (1992) 'Schizophrenia: manifestations, incidence and course in different cultures: A World Health Organization ten-country study.' *Psychological Medicine Monograph Supplement 21*, 1–97.

Joffe, A. and Yancy, W. (2004) 'Legalization of marijuana: potential impact on youth.' *Pediatrics 113*, 632–638.

Johnston, L., O'Malley, P. and Bachman, J. (1981) *Marijuana Decriminalization: The Impact on Youth 1975–1980. Monitoring the Future.* Occasional paper 13. Ann Arbor, MI: Institute for Social Research, University of Michigan.

Jones, S. and Heaven, P. (1998) 'Psychosocial correlates of adolescent drug-taking behaviour.' *Journal of Adolescence 21*, 127–134.

Kandel D. and Chen, K. (2000) 'Types of marijuana users by longitudinal course.' *Journal of Studies on Alcohol 61*, 367–378.

Kandel, D. and Davies, M. (1986) 'Adult sequelae of adolescent depressive symptoms.' *Archives of General Psychiatry 43*, 255–262.

Kandel, D., Davies, M., Karus, D. and Yamaguchi, K. (1986) 'The consequences in young adulthood of adolescent drug involvement.' *Archives of General Psychiatry 43*, 746–754.

Kandel, D., Yamaguchi, K. and Chen, K. (1992) 'Stages of progression in drug involvement from adolescence to adulthood: further evidence for the gateway theory.' *Journal of Studies on Alcohol 53*, 447–457.

Kendell, R. (2003) 'Cannabis condemned: the proscription of Indian hemp.' *Addiction 98*, 143–151.

Khan, K., Kunz, R., Kleijnen, J. and Antes, G. (2003) *Systematic Reviews to Support Evidence-based Medicine.* London: Royal Society of Medicine Press.

Korf, D. (2002) 'Dutch coffee shops and trends in cannabis use.' *Addictive Behaviors 27*, 851–866.

Krohn, M., Lizotte, A. and Perez, C. (1997) 'The interrelationship between substance use and precocious transitions to adult statuses.' *Journal of Health and Social Behavior 38*, 87–103.

Lachner, G., Wittchen, H.-U., Perkonigg, A., Holly, A., Schuster, P., Wunderlich, U. *et al.* (1998) 'Structure, content and reliability of the Munich-Composite International Diagnostic Interview (M-CIDI) substance use sections.' *European Addiction Research 4*, 28–41.

Lewis, G. and Pelosi, A. (1992) *The Manual of CIS-R.* London: Institute of Psychiatry.

Linszen, D., Dingemans, P. and Lenior, M. (1994) 'Cannabis abuse and the course of recent-onset schizophrenic disorders.' *Archives of General Psychiatry 51*, 273–279.

Lloyd, C. (1998) 'Risk factors for problem drug use: identifying vulnerable groups.' *Drugs: Education, Prevention and Policy 5*, 217–232.

Lynskey, M., Coffey, C., Degenhardt, L., Carlin, J. and Patton, G. (2003) 'A longitudinal study of the effects of adolescent cannabis use on high school completion.' *Addiction 98*, 685–692.

Lynskey, M. and Hall, W. (2000) 'The effects of adolescent cannabis use on educational attainment: a review.' *Addiction 95*, 1621–1630.

MacCoun, R. (1998) 'In what sense (if any) is marijuana a gateway drug? *FAS Drug Policy Analysis, Issue 4, February.* http://fas.org/drugs

MacCoun, R. and Reuter, P. (2001) 'Evaluating alternative cannabis regimes.' *British Journal of Psychiatry 178*, 123–128.

Macleod, J., Oakes, R., Copello, A., Crome, I., Egger, M., Hickman, M., Oppenkowski, T., Stokes-Lampard, H. and Davey Smith, G. (2004) 'Psychological and social sequelae of cannabis and other illicit drug use by young people: a systematic review of longitudinal, general population studies.' *Lancet 363*, 1579–1588.

Maine Office of Alcoholism and Drug Abuse Prevention (1979) *An Evaluation of the Decriminalization of Marijuana in Maine*. Augusta, ME: Office of Alcoholism and Drug Prevention.

McCambridge, J. and Strang, J. (2004a) 'Patterns of drug use in a sample of 200 young drug users in London.' *Drugs: Education, Prevention and Policy, 11*, 101–112.

McCambridge, J. and Strang, J. (2004b) 'The efficacy of single-session motivational interviewing in reducing drug consumption and perceptions of drug-related risk and harm among young people: results from a multi-site cluster randomized trial.' *Addiction 99*, 39–52.

McGee, R., Williams, S., Poulton, R. and Moffitt, T. (2000) 'A longitudinal study of cannabis use and mental health from adolescence to early adulthood.' *Addiction 95*, 491–503.

McGlothin, W. and West, L. (1968) 'The marijuana problem: an overview.' *American Journal of Psychiatry 125*, 370–378.

McIntosh, J., MacDonald, F. and McKeganey, N. (2003) 'Knowledge and perceptions of illegal drugs in a sample of pre-teenage children.' *Drugs: Education, Prevention and Policy 10*, 331–344.

McVie, S., Campbell, S. and Lebov, K. (2004) *Scottish Crime Survey 2003*. Edinburgh: Scottish Executive Social Research.

Mensch, B. and Kandel, K. (1988) 'Dropping-out of high school and drug involvement.' *Sociology of Education 61*, 95–113.

Miller, P. and Plant, M. (1999) 'Truancy and perceived school performance: an alcohol and drug study of UK teenagers.' *Alcohol and Alcoholism 34*, 886–893.

Miller, T. and Volk, R. (1996) 'Weekly marijuana use as a risk factor for initial cocaine use: results from a six-wave national survey.' *Journal of Child and Adolescent Substance Abuse 5*, 55–78.

Miller-Johnson, S., Lochman, J., Coie, J., Terry, R. and Hyman, C. (1998) 'Comorbidity of conduct and depressive problems at sixth grade: substance use outcomes across adolescence.' *Journal of Abnormal Child Psychology 26*, 221–232.

Moffitt, T. and Silva, P. (1988) 'Self-reported delinquency: results from an instrument for New Zealand.' *Australian and New Zealand Journal of Criminology 21*, 227–240.

MORI Social Research (1999) *Drugs Report: A Research Study among 11–16 year olds. Research Study Conducted for the Police Foundation, January–February.* London: MORI.

Morrall, A., McCaffrey, D. and Paddock, S. (2002) 'Reassessing the marijuana gateway effect.' *Addiction 97*, 1493–1504.

NACD and DAIRU (National Advisory Committee on Drugs and Drug and Alcohol Information and Research Unit) (2003) *Drug Use in Ireland and Northern Ireland: First Results from the 2002/2003 Drug Prevalence Survey.* www.nacd.ie

Negrete, J., Knapp, W., Douglas, D. and Smith, W. (1986) 'Cannabis affects the severity of schizophrenic symptoms: results of a clinical survey.' *Psychological Medicine 16*, 515–520.

Novins, D. and Mitchell, C. (1998) 'Factors associated with marijuana use among American Indian adolescents.' *Addiction 93*, 1693–1702.

Overall, J. and Gorham, D. (1962) 'The Brief Psychiatric Rating Scale.' *Psychological Reports 10*, 799–812.

Palmgreen, P., Donohew, L., Lorch, E., Hoyle, R. and Stephenson, M. (2001) 'Television campaigns and adolescent marijuana use: tests of sensation seeking targeting.' *American Journal of Public Health 91*, 292–296.

Paton, S., Kessler, R. and Kandel, D. (1977) 'Depressive mood and adolescent illicit drug use: a longitudinal analysis.' *Journal of Genetic Psychology 131*, 267–289.

Patton, G., Coffey, C., Carlin, J., Degenhardt, L., Lynskey, M. and Hall, W. (2002) 'Cannabis use and mental health in young people: cohort study.' *British Medical Journal 325*, 1195–1198.

Pearson, G. and Shiner, M. (2002) 'Rethinking the generation gap: attitudes to illicit drugs among young people and adults.' *Criminal Justice 2*, 71–86.

Pedersen, W., Mastekaasa, A. and Wichstrom, L. (2001) 'Conduct problems and early cannabis initiation: a longitudinal study of gender differences.' *Addiction 96*, 415–431.

Perkonigg, A., Lieb, R., Hofler, M., Schuster, P., Sonntag, H. and Wittchen, H.-U. (1999) 'Patterns of cannabis use, abuse and dependence over time: incidence, progression and stability in a sample of 1228 adolescents.' *Addiction 94*, 1663–1678.

Police Foundation (2000) *Drugs and the Law: Report of the Independent Inquiry into the Misuse of Drugs Act 1971*. London: Police Foundation.

Poulton, R., Brooke, M., Moffitt, T., Stanton, W. and Silva, P. (1997) 'Prevalence and correlates of cannabis use and dependence in young New Zealanders.' *New Zealand Medical Journal 110*, 68–70.

Quay, H. and Peterson, D. (1987) *Manual for the Revised Behavior Problem Checklist*. Miami, FL: University of Miami.

Regier, D., Farmer, M., Rae, D., Locker, B., Keith, B., Judd, L. *et al.* (1990) 'Comorbidity of mental disorders with alcohol and other drug abuse: results from the epidemiologic catchment area (ECA) study.' *Journal of the American Medical Association 264*, 2511–2518.

Reinarman, C., Cohen, P. and Kaal, H. (2004) 'The limited relevance of drug policy: cannabis in Amsterdam and in San Francisco.' *American Journal of Public Health 94*, 836–842.

Resnick, M., Bearman, P., Blum, R., Bauman, K., Harris, K., Jones, J., Tabor, J., Beuhring, T., Sieving, R., Shew, M., Ireland, M., Bearinger, L. and Udry, J. (1997) 'Protecting adolescents from harm: findings from the National Longitudinal Study on Adolescent Health.' *Journal of the American Medical Association 278*, 823–832.

Rey, J., Martin, A. and Krabman, P. (2004) 'Is the party over? Cannabis and juvenile psychiatric disorder: the past 10 years.' *Journal of the American Academy of Child and Adolescent Psychiatry 43*, 1194–1205.

Rey, J., Sawyer, M., Raphael, B., Patton, G. and Lynskey, M. (2002) 'Mental health of teenagers who use cannabis: results of an Australian survey.' *British Journal of Psychiatry 180*, 216–221.

Robins, L. and Regier, D. (1991) *Psychiatric Disorders in America: The Epidemiologic Catchment Area Study*. New York: The Free Press.

Rodham, K., Hawton, K., Evans, E. and Weatherall, R. (2005) 'Ethnic and gender differences in drinking, smoking and drug taking among adolescents in England: a self-report school-based survey of 15 and 16 year olds.' *Journal of Adolescence 28*, 63–73.

Rogers, A. and McCarthy, M. (1999) 'Drugs and drugs education in the inner city: the views of 12-year-olds and their parents.' *Drugs: Education, Prevention and Policy 6*, 51–59.

Rosenbaum, E. and Kandel, D. (1990) 'Early onset of adolescent sexual behaviour and drug involvement.' *Journal of Marriage and the Family 52*, 783–798.

SAMHSA (Substance Abuse and Mental Health Services Administration) *Adult Marijuana Admissions by Race and Ethnicity: 2000. The Oasis Report (p.1)*. Rockville, MD: Office for Applied Statistics.

Saveland, W. and Bray, D. (1980) *American Trends in Cannabis Use among States with Different and Changing Legal Regimes*. Ottawa, Canada: Bureau of Tobacco and Control and Biometrics, Health and Welfare.

Silva, P. and Stanton, W. (eds) (1996) *From Child to Adult: The Dunedin Multidisciplinary Health and Development Study*. Auckland: Oxford University Press.

Single, E., Christie, P. and Ali, R. (2000) 'The impact of cannabis decriminalisation in Australia and the United States.' *Journal of Public Health Policy 21*, 157–186.

Smeets, R. and Dingemans, P. (1993) *Composite International Diagnostic Interview (CIDI): Version 1.1.* Geneva, Switzerland: World Health Organization.

Smit, F., Bolier, L. and Cuijpers, P. (2004) 'Cannabis use and the risk of later schizophrenia: a review.' *Addiction 99*, 425–430.

Smith, D. (1968) 'Acute and chronic toxicity of marijuana.' *Journal of Psychedelic Drugs 2*, 37–47.

Smith, N. (2002) 'A review of the published literature into cannabis withdrawal symptoms in human users.' *Addiction 97*, 621–632.

Solowij, N. (1999) 'Long term effects of cannabis on the nervous system.' In H. Kalant, W. Corigall, W. Hall and R. Smart (eds) *The Health Effects of Cannabis.* Toronto, Canada: Addiction Research Foundation.

Spitzner, J. (1979) *Drug Use in Ohio: 1978.* Columbus, OH: Ohio Bureau of Drug Abuse.

Stephenson, M., Palmgreen, P., Hoyle, R., Donohew, L., Lorch, E. and Colon, S. (1999) 'Short-term effects of an anti-marijuana media campaign targeting high sensation seeking adolescents.' *Journal of Applied Communication Research 27*, 175–195.

Stevens, M., Freeman, D., Mott, L. and Youells, F. (1996) 'Three-year results of prevention programs: the New Hampshire study.' *Journal of Drug Education 26*, 257–273.

Stevens, M., Freeman, D., Mott, L., Youells, F. and Linsey, S. (1993) 'Smokeless tobacco use among children: the New Hampshire study.' *American Journal of Preventive Medicine 9*, 160–167.

Sussmann, S. and Dent, C. (1999) 'One-year prospective prediction of marijuana use cessation among youth at continuation high schools.' *Addictive Behaviors 24*, 411–417.

Sussmann, S. and Dent, C. (2004) 'Five-year prospective prediction of marijuana use cessation of youth at continuation high school.' *Addictive Behaviors 29*, 1237–1243.

Swift, W., Copeland, J., Howard, J., Roffman, R., Stephens, R. and Berghuis, J. (2001) 'Adolescent cannabis check-up and intervention trial.' *Drug and Alcohol Dependence 63*, s156.

Tien, A. and Anthony, J. (1990) 'Epidemiological analysis of alcohol and drug use as risk factors for psychotic experiences.' *Journal of Nervous and Mental Disease 178*, 473–480.

Tobler, N., Lessard, T., Marshall, D., Ochshorn, P. and Roona, M. (1999) 'Effectiveness of school-based drug prevention programs for marijuana use.' *School Psychology International 20*, 105–137.

UN ODCCP (United Nations Office for Drug Control and Crime Prevention) (2000) *Demand Reduction: A Glossary of Terms.* New York: United Nations.

US SAMHSA (United States Substance Abuse and Mental Health Service Administration) (2000) *National Household Survey on Drug Abuse: Main Findings 1998.* Rockville, MD: United States Department of Health and Human Services.

Van den Bree, M. and Pickworth, W. (2005) 'Risk factors predicting changes in marijuana involvement in teenagers.' *Archives of General Psychiatry 62*, 311–319.

Van Os, J., Bak, M., Hanssen, M., Bijl, R., de Graaf, R. and Verdoux, H. (2002) 'Cannabis use and psychosis: a longitudinal population-based study.' *American Journal of Epidemiology 156*, 319–327.

Verdoux, H. and Tournier, M. (2004) 'Cannabis use and risk of psychosis: an etiological link?' *Epidemiologia e Psichiatria Sociale 13*, 113–119.

Waldron, H., Slesnick, N., Brody, J., Turner, C. and Peterson, T. (2001) 'Treatment outcomes for adolescent substance abuse at 4- and 7-month assessments.' *Journal of Consulting and Clinical Psychology 69*, 802–813.

Warner, J., Weber, T. and Albanes, R. (1999) '"Girls are retarded when they're stoned." Marijuana and the construction of gender roles among adolescent females.' *Sex Roles 40*, 25–43.

Weiser, M., Knobler, H., Noy, S. and Kaplan, Z. (2002) 'Clinical characteristics of adolescents later hospitalized for schizophrenia.' *American Journal of Medical Genetics 114*, 949–955.

Weissman, M., Wolk, S., Wickramaratne, P., Goldstein, R., Adams, P., Greenwald, S., Ryan, N., Dahl, R. and Steinberg, D. (1999) 'Children with prepubertal-onset major depressive disorder and anxiety grown up.' *Archives of General Psychiatry 56*, 794–801.

White, A., Jordan, J., Schroeder, K., Acheson, S., Georgi, B., Sauls, G. *et al.* (2004) 'Predictors of relapse during treatment and treatment completion among marijuana-dependent adolescents in an intensive outpatient substance abuse program.' *Substance Abuse 25*, 53–59.

White, D. and Pitts, M. (1998) 'Educating young people about drugs: a systematic review.' *Addiction 93*, 1475–1487.

Wibberley, C. and Price, J. (2000) 'Young people's drug use: facts and feelings – implications for the normalization debate.' *Drugs: Education, Prevention and Policy 7*, 147–162.

Wincup, E., Buckland, G. and Bayliss, R. (2003) *Youth Homelessness and Substance Use: Report to the Drugs and Alcohol Research Unit.* London: Home Office.

Windle, M. and Wiesner, M. (2004) 'Trajectories of marijuana use from adolescence to young adulthood: predictors and outcomes.' *Development and Psychopathology 16*, 1007–1027.

Wittchen, H.-U., Lachner, G., Wunderlich, U. and Pfister, H. (1998a) 'Test-retest reliability of the computerised DSM-IV version of the Munich-Composite International Diagnostic Interview (M-CIDI).' *Social Psychiatry and Psychiatric Epidemiology 33*, 568–578.

Wittchen, H.-U., Perkonigg, A., Lachner, G. and Nelson, C. (1998b) 'Early developmental stages of psychopathology study (EDSP): objectives and design.' *European Addiction Research 4*, 18–27.

Wodak, A., Reinarman, C., Cohen, P. and Drummond, C. (2002) 'For and against. Cannabis control: costs outweigh the benefits.' *British Medical Journal 324*, 105–108.

World Health Organization (WHO) (1974) *Glossary of Mental Health Disorders and Guide to their Classification for Use in Conjunction with International Classification of Diseases* 8th revision. Geneva: WHO.

WHO (1992) *International Statistical Classification of Diseases and Related Health Problems* 10th edn. Geneva: WHO.

WHO (1993) *Composite International Diagnostic Interview (CIDI).* Geneva: WHO.

Zammit, S., Allebeck, P., Andreasson, S., Lundberg, I. and Lewis, G. (2002) 'Self reported cannabis use as a risk factor for schizophrenia in Swedish conscripts of 1969: historical cohort study.' *British Medical Journal 325*, 1199–1201.

Zimmermann, P., Muhlig, S., Sonntag, D., Buhringer, G. and Wittchen, H.-U. (2004) 'Review on psychotherapeutic interventions for cannabis disorders.' *Sucht 50*, 334–342.

Zuckerman, M. (1994) *Behavioral Expression and Biosocial Bases of Sensation Seeking.* New York, NY: Cambridge University Press.

Subject Index

Author Index

About Focus

FOCUS was launched in 1997 to promote clinical and organisational effectiveness in child and adolescent mental health services, with an emphasis on incorporating evidence-based research into everyday practice.

Please visit our website to find out more about our work (including our discussion forum and conferences): www.focusproject.org.uk